MY POCKET

GUIDE

~ TO ~

MANIFESTATION

MY POCKET

GUIDE

~ TO ~

MANIFESTATION

ANYTIME ACTIVITIES TO SET INTENTIONS, VISUALIZE
GOALS, AND CREATE THE LIFE YOU WANT

KELSEY AIDA ROUALDES

Adams Media
New York London Toronto Sydney New Delhi

Adams Media
An Imprint of Simon & Schuster, Inc.
100 Technology Center Drive
Stoughton, Massachusetts 02072

First Adams Media trade paperback edition May 2022

ADAMS MEDIA and colophon are trademarks of Simon & Schuster.

For information about special discounts for bulk purchases, please contact Simon & Schuster Special Sales at 1-866-506-1949 or business@simonandschuster.com.

The Simon & Schuster Speakers Bureau can bring authors to your live event. For more information or to book an event contact the Simon & Schuster Speakers Bureau at 1-866-248-3049 or visit our website at www.simonspeakers.com.

Interior design by Michelle Kelly
Images © 123RF/Ekaterina Matveeva

Manufactured in China

10 9 8 7 6 5 4 3 2 1

Library of Congress Cataloging-in-Publication Data has been applied for.

ISBN 978-1-5072-1830-3
ISBN 978-1-5072-1831-0 (ebook)

CONTENTS

PART 1:
MANIFESTING BASICS / 11

PART 2:
MANIFESTING YOUR DESIRES / 25

INTRODUCTION

Do you want to live a more creative and intentional life?
Are you looking to experience your own power in action?
Are you ready to turn your dreams and desires into
your new and improved reality?

If so, it's time to leverage your own creative abilities and start manifesting!

Manifesting is the act of turning thoughts into things and bringing your dreams into reality through the powers of *desire, imagination, focus,* and *alignment.* Here's how it works: A *desire* arises within you and you set an intention to experience it one day. Then you spend some time *focusing* on what you want in a relaxed and *imaginative* way. Lastly, you make the appropriate adjustments to your life, thoughts, beliefs, and actions in order to *align* your energy with the energy of your desire. And soon enough, with a little help from the Universe, something that was once just an idea in your mind becomes your new reality! This is the power of manifestation.

My Pocket Guide to Manifestation presents nearly one hundred fun and effective manifesting exercises you can do at home, at work, or on the go to help you create a life you love, one intention at a time. These simple but powerful manifestation techniques will help you live more intentionally, co-create with the Universe, and improve your life in any of the following areas:

* Love
* Financial Abundance
* Vibrant Health
* Beneficial Relationships

* Happiness
* Peace
* Purpose

While the basics of manifestation are simple to practice, everyone runs into obstacles along the way. That's why *My Pocket Guide to Manifestation* will teach you how to release *resistance*, which can hold you back from getting what you want. Releasing resistance will help you get all of your energy flowing in the same direction, so you can manifest with fewer blockages and more ease!

Allow this book to be your manifestation partner whenever you feel the urge to create something new or improve some facet of your life. Feel free to work through these exercises in whatever order feels the best for you—you can start with one that resonates with you right now, then follow your inspiration from there. You can also come back to revisit your favorite exercises and personalize them to your preferences. This is your manifestation practice. Play with it and make it your own!

Whether you're looking to find your soul mate, boost your income, or simply embrace more happiness, this book is for you. There's no time like the present to begin living the life you want, so let's get manifesting!

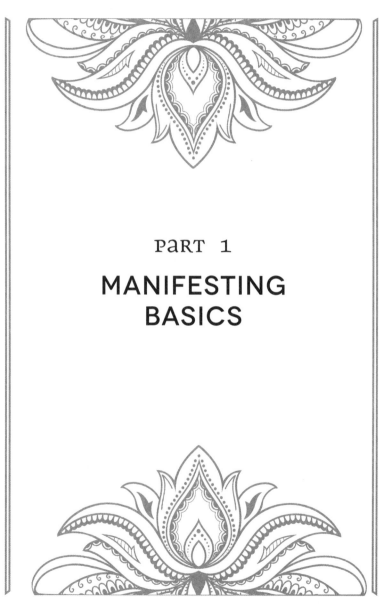

PART 1

MANIFESTING BASICS

CHAPTER 1

UNDERSTANDING MANIFESTATION

The process of manifesting your desires is very simple at its root: You'll focus your intentions and energy on your goal and aim to live in alignment with the energies, thoughts, and actions that will support it. This chapter will outline exactly why and how this process works and explain how you can integrate manifestation into your daily life with the exercises in this book. You'll also learn how to overcome the normal types of resistance you're likely to encounter along the way. It's all part of your journey to the life you want.

WHAT ARE MANIFESTING METHODS?

A manifesting method is any technique, practice, ritual, or exercise that you do in order to get something you want. It usually involves some sort of intention setting, visualization, deliberate focus, energy work, or resistance release. The exercises in this book feature easy-to-follow manifesting methods that you can do anytime, anywhere to help you realize your desires.

Each exercise is designed with a specific beneficial outcome in mind. Generally speaking, the more focused your goals are, the better manifestation works.

For example, some exercises (like Discover What You Really Want Financially) will help you to gain clarity about what you specifically want and why you want it so that you can more easily achieve it. Some exercises (such as Manifest Amazing Love with a Meditation) will help you visualize your desire from different angles to help you line up with it. Others (like Release Blockages to Manifesting Your Health) will help you release any limiting beliefs or energetic blockages you may have that have been holding you back from experiencing what you want. And some (such as Tune In to Happiness via Sights and Sounds) will help you become a vibrational match to what you are asking for via different energetic modalities. What they all have in common is that each one will bring you closer to realizing your dream, whatever it may be!

THE UNIVERSE WANTS WHAT YOU WANT

To manifest your desires, you'll be working hand in hand with the Universe. After all, from a spiritual and energetic perspective, you are a fractal of the Universe.

You Are the Universe

You are made up of the same elements as the stars, rocks, plants, air, energy, ocean...everything! Quite literally, you *are* the Universe. And the Universe is *you*. Since you are a part of the Universe, the creative consciousness of the Universe is acting *as* you and *through* you all the time to discover more about itself and expand itself. The way it does this is primarily through *thought* and *desire*. Just like you, the Universe wants to know itself...create new things...learn...and expand in all directions.

Even though it doesn't always feel like it, the Universe actually wants what you want. Because you are it and it is you. How could your desire be separate from that of the Universe if you are one? It's not! Your desire *is* the Universe's desire and vice versa. That's why whenever you genuinely want something, the Universe provides it for you. Sure, it might not look exactly how you thought it would, but the feeling flavor will always be there.

When you think a new thought or have a new desire, the Universe's consciousness expands through yours. And when you eventually get what you want, that opens up space for you to want more, which leads to even more expansion! That's why it's always in the Universe's best interest for you to get what you want. You're the ultimate team for Universal expansion and growth!

It's Not Selfish to Want Something

Desire gets a bad rep in some parts of the spiritual community for being "selfish," but desire is actually the main vehicle for expansion—both your personal expansion and that of the Universe. Without it, nothing new would be created, grow, progress, or move forward. Therefore, desire is extremely important and something that's beneficial for you to work with, rather than try to suppress or deny.

In fact, desires and destiny are naturally intertwined, because your desires *are* your destiny. Consider this: We usually think of manifesting as creating something new, but what if your desires are really just *premonitions* of what's to come? What if your desires are simply letting you know what's next on the list for you to experience? If you genuinely want something, there is a good reason why: It's meant to be! And if it's not meant to be, the desire will most likely fade away or evolve into something better. Either way, desire is something to follow in order to be on your highest path.

It's not bad or wrong to want things. It's normal, natural, and perfectly human to want to experience something new or something more! In the process, you discover things you like and things you don't, and with each bit of clarity comes new desires. To make yourself feel bad or wrong for genuinely wanting something is to suppress your own life force energy and go against the very forces of nature that you came here to express.

Deciding what you want to be...do...have...feel...this is all what you came here to do in this life. So don't be shy. Lean into your creative abilities and work your magic! You are destined to experience what you want in one form or another, so you may as well get your hands dirty and have some fun with the process. Use this book to help you validate and honor your desires. Whoever tells you not to pursue your genuine desires has sadly lost touch with theirs. Simply send them love and light and then go live your best life, desires and all!

HOW DOES MANIFESTING WORK?

All matter, including you, is made up of energy. It's been proven time and time again, through the nature of life itself and even through quantum physics, that your thoughts, your energy, and your intentions affect energy. Therefore, you have the ability to influence your reality, sway circumstances, and create specific experiences.

This world of cause and effect is ruled by the Law of Attraction. Sometimes called the Law of Mirroring, it states that like energy attracts like energy. This means that your energy is a vibrational match to certain experiences, circumstances, and outcomes. Changing that energy through manifestation techniques like the exercises in this book can change your vibration and change your outcomes.

How Manifesting and the Law of Attraction Work, in Three Simple Steps

The Law of Attraction works like this:

1. You desire something.
2. The Universe responds to that desire by creating it (for you and *through* you).
3. When you're ready (a.k.a., when you're a vibrational match to your desire), you'll receive it!

Let's break down each step a little further.

Step 1: Your Desire

Your life experience is always causing you to birth new desires, usually through some kind of adversity or undesirable circumstance, or even just a clarified personal preference. This a normal and natural part of the human experience that doesn't require any effort on your part. It's when you claim your desire and declare something along the lines of:

* *Hey, Universe! This is what I want to experience next.*
* *It would be amazing if _____ happened!*
* *I would love to do, be, or have _____.*

Once you have identified a personal desire, ask yourself *why* you want what you want. Usually, you will discover that you're really after a *feeling*. The deepest reason that you ever want anything is because you believe you will feel differently or better when you have it. Knowing your "why" will help you discover your *genuine* desire (how you want to feel); then you'll become a vibrational match to what you want to experience. Feeling how you ultimately want to feel *now*, instead of waiting for certain circumstances to be met first, is how to line up energetically with your desires, which will manifest them faster. For example, when you're already thankful, you are a vibrational match to experiencing more things to be thankful for!

Step 2: The Universe Responds

When you want something, the Universe starts arranging and rearranging things, people, and circumstances on your behalf to aid in the creation of your desire. This is the part where faith and belief come in handy! When you believe that what you want is possible and you have faith in the ability of yourself and the Universe to deliver it, you will have less resistance, which will help your manifesting efforts. And if you don't believe or have faith yet, start questioning the limiting stories you are telling yourself. Can you know for certain that they are true?

Step 3: Manifestation

Lastly, there's "the work" or "the wait," depending on what you're manifesting and how much or little resistance you are practicing. The work is how you participate in your creation by taking action, be it energetically or in the physical world. It may involve upgrading your habits, thoughts, beliefs, consciousness, or mood. You may also need to discover and release any resistance you have concerning where you are or what you want. (More on how to do this later.) And it will definitely be helpful to act on any inspiration that comes to you during this time. The wait is all about living your best life in the meantime while your manifestation is coming together behind the scenes. Instead of doing what most people do, which is constantly notice the absence of their desire, you assume that your wish is already granted and you move on with your life without obsessing over outcomes. This casual and cool approach always works well when manifesting. Because if you're enjoying your life now, you'll just keep attracting more things and experiences to enjoy!

After enough time has passed for your desire to be created perfectly and for you to become a vibrational match to it, you will receive it and finally enjoy the fruits of your creation! This can happen almost instantaneously or after a prolonged period of time. There are many factors at play, so it just depends. Understandably, the end is the part we all want to skip ahead to. But as corny as it sounds, the majority of your satisfaction really is in the journey.

While it is super fun to get what you want, most of your true satisfaction lies in the creative process itself: when you first get inspired by the desire, every time you daydream about it, when you take the steps to go after it, whenever you tell your friends about it, and especially when you become the new and improved version of yourself. This is the manifestation journey. This is what it's all about!

Enjoy the Process

As you work through this book, enjoy the process and have fun! Effective manifesting methods work because they help you align your energy with your desires so you can become a match to the things you want to experience in this life. Each time you do an exercise in this book, you will utilize your imagination, time, focus, and energy to create energetic momentum to manifest your desires. And remember: No dream is too big, too weird, or too selfish. As long as you're not using your power to hurt yourself or anyone else in the process, you've got the green light! When it's a *genuine* desire, you owe it to yourself and the world to go for it!

WHEN IS THE BEST TIME TO DO THESE EXERCISES?

The best time to practice manifestation is when you're in a good, light, playful, imaginative, excited, calm, focused, or hopeful mood. Trying to do these exercises from a place of desperation or thoughts of lack will not yield great results, as your energy will be off and your thoughts are not focused on abundance when you feel like this. Instead, try these activities when you are feeling inspired or generally good about what you are wanting to create.

Every time a new desire pops into your mind, reference this book and utilize the appropriate exercises. And if you want to manifest something that isn't mentioned in the book, use the exercises as inspiration to create your own manifesting processes. Manifestation is all about imagination, so feel free to get creative.

UNDERSTANDING AND OVERCOMING RESISTANCE

Let's say you are trying to manifest something, but you feel stuck or you're not getting the results that you had hoped for. There's usually only one thing that's holding you back: resistance.

What Is Resistance?

Resistance is split energy, when some of your energy is encouraging the creation of your desire and some of your energy is working against it. It's any oppositional force that creates a stalemate. This situation may well be happening on a subconscious level, so you may not recognize it at first. Luckily for you, this book has plenty of tools to help you uncover any hidden resistance you may have so you can consciously work to resolve it.

Identifying Your Resistance

In order to overcome resistance, you must bring it into your awareness and deal with it directly to create less opposition and more alignment. The first step is to know what resistance looks and feels like for you. Once you've identified what the resistance is, then you can work to dissolve, release, or transmute it accordingly. (Don't worry, you'll find many ideas for overcoming resistance in the exercises in this book.)

Resistance can show up in many forms, but you can tell that you are carrying some form of resistance when you feel closed, stuck, scared, hesitant, or anything similar. You may notice resistance in your life in general, or you may find it in certain areas of life or pertaining to certain things that you want.

Here are some common examples of what resistance may look like:

* Resisting yourself: When different parts of you want different things. For example, part of you wants to move to a new city to accept your dream job, but another part of you wants to stay close to family, keeping you stuck.
* Resisting your desire: Being scared or hesitant to get what you want. For example, you want to ask someone out on a date, but you've been burned and rejected so many times that you don't even try.
* Resisting a perceived threat: Any and all forms of self-sabotage. You may be on the brink of hitting a big personal

goal, but you blow it at the last minute because a part of you thinks it would be somehow bad for you to achieve it.

* Resisting your feelings: You suppress, deny, or disown how you feel. For example, you pretend that everything is fine, even when it's not.

* Resisting your life: You don't accept your current reality. You refuse to embrace your life or make the best of where you are because you think that if you do you are settling and will get stuck.

* Limiting beliefs: Words, thoughts, or actions that contradict what you want. For instance, you say and feel that you want more money, but you believe money is the root of all evil, and you obviously don't want to be evil, so you subconsciously push money away.

* Interference of other people or circumstances that are going against what you want (which is just an outward reflection of your internal resistance): For example, you want the house to be clean, but your kids refuse to pick up their rooms.

Once you've identified what your resistance is, it's time to resolve it to create some alignment and get things moving forward.

Moving Past Resistance

Most people try to ignore resistance, go around it, or bulldoze right over it. These options don't work, though—when you do this, you are simply resisting your resistance, which just creates more of the same! As the saying goes, "What you resist persists."

Resolving resistance can look different for everyone under different circumstances, but the general rule is to use genuine curiosity and compassion as tools. You have to assume that the resistance has a good reason for being there; approach it as you would a friend who is in pain. Listen to your resistance, validate it, and bring compassion to it in order to resolve it. Who knows, it may just be pointing you to deeper desire or personal truth that you may not have been aware of before!

Often, just becoming aware of your resistance is enough for it to stop being a problem for you. You might experience awareness in one of these forms:

* Realizing that your limiting belief just isn't true or serving you anymore.
* Embracing a feeling you've been suppressing for years so it can finally heal itself.
* Seeing how you've been holding yourself back and deciding to try something different this time.

The possibilities for resolution and progress are endless once you simply become aware of your resistance!

But if/when realizing the resistance isn't enough, there are many more creative ways you can heal it through methods such as:

* Therapy
* Life coaching
* Journaling
* Self-inquiry or contemplation
* Meditation
* Hypnosis

As with any life skill, it takes practice to overcome your resistance, but luckily you'll get lots in the following pages.

Once you untangle your resistance, all your energy can move in the same direction to support your desire(s). The people who are the most successful at realizing their dreams in life are the ones who can untangle resistance and create resolve within. After all, the Law of Attraction states, "As within, so without." Resolve your inner world, and everything in your outer world will start to fall into place.

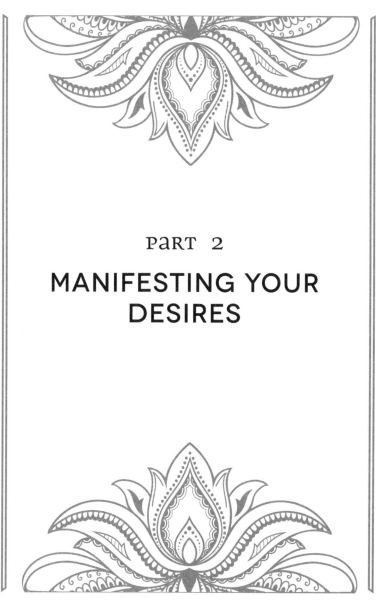

PART 2

MANIFESTING YOUR DESIRES

CHAPTER 2

MANIFESTING LOVE

This chapter will help you manifest all things love, partnership, and romance! Whether you're already in a relationship that you want to improve or you're ready to meet the love of your life, the activities that follow will help make you a vibrational match to the type of love you've been dreaming of.

As you embark on your love-manifesting journey, it's best to...

* Get specific about how your future relationship will *feel*, but stay open to *whom* it will be with.
* Remember that your person is out there somewhere also wishing and wanting to be with someone just like you!

* Become your own soul mate first. (It's the fastest way to manifest one!)
* Realize that love, companionship, and romance are all naturally occurring human experiences that are readily available for those who are ready to receive them.

Now, let's get started. Love awaits!

Identify Your Genuine Desires in Love

Knowing *why* you want love will help you go after what you truly desire in a more direct and intentional way. This will give you great clarity as to exactly what you're looking for and will help you become a vibrational match to your dream relationship in the process. It's a win-win scenario. Here's how:

1. Ask yourself *why* you want to manifest love/a relationship. If necessary, keep asking yourself why over and over until you narrow it down to a few core feelings. For example, you may realize, *I want to manifest love so I can feel safe, cherished, adored.*

2. Focus your thoughts, feelings, decisions, actions, and life in a way that helps you cultivate the feelings you want to experience in your future love life right now. For example, if you want to feel safe, cherished, and adored, how can you start helping yourself feel these ways right now? To assist you with this step, ask yourself these two questions and write down whatever comes to you:

   * What's stopping me from feeling how I want to feel right now?
   * How can I feel more of how I want to feel until the relationship comes?

3. Use your discoveries from steps one and two to make empowering adjustments to your daily life so that you can start feeling more of how you want to feel today! For example, you may realize that you never take that time to adore or cherish yourself, so you make a habit of doing so in the little ways that you can.

This activity will give you the clarity and the road map to helping your lover show up in no time!

Journal Your Love Into Existence

When you're in an awesome relationship, it looks and feels certain ways—but when you're on your own, it can be difficult to recapture those feelings. In this exercise you'll re-familiarize yourself with that experience by daydreaming about what your future relationship will be, then writing it down on paper. When you do this, not only are you giving the Universe some specific intel to work with, but you are also spending time focusing on your desire in a positive, nonattached way, which will lead you to create more supportive energy around it.

Here are a few pointers before you begin your journal entry:

* Write in the *present tense*, as if your dream reality were already a fact.
* Use *specifics* to make it feel more real to you.
* Emphasize how you are *feeling* in this future reality.
* Use a real pen/pencil and paper to write the entry by hand.
* Don't limit the Universe by planning exactly *how* and *when* this will all come about.

Now imagine your dream love outcome and write it down as if it were already your reality. Take yourself there in your mind and on paper!

Here are some phrases to help you:

* My relationship makes me feel...
* My love and I do these types of fun things together...
* I'm happy that we...
* I'm grateful for a partner who...

Expect powerful change to happen when you put pen to paper. Later you can come back to this entry and be amazed at how much of it has come true!

Manifest Amazing Love with a Meditation

The more time you spend being "in love"—whether it be with your life, yourself, or your dog—the more you become a vibrational match to manifesting all types of love, including the romantic kind. In this meditation, you will take an energetic love "bath" in order to do just that. Follow these steps:

1. Sit or lie down comfortably. Close your eyes, lengthen your spine, uncross your limbs, and turn your palms up.
2. Breathe slowly and deeply for a few minutes, focusing on opening your heart and cultivating a strong feeling of love. Think of something or someone you love more than anything to connect to the feeling of love in your mind and body. Do this for at least one minute to gain some energetic traction.
3. As you feel this love grow inside of you, imagine: What color is its energy? What would it look like if it were an object? What does it sound like? What is the texture and consistency of this love? How does it feel in your body? Observe everything you can about it.
4. Starting with your chest, feel this love slowly expand up and down into the rest of your body. With each breath, see and feel this energy fill up more and more of your being. Let the love come over every single part of your body until you are completely full. Stay here for as long as it feels good.

This exercise helps you *feel* in love now. The more time you spend bathing in love, the easier love will come to you!

Reconcile Your Ambivalence

If some parts of you want to be in love, but others don't, not much will manifest. That's why it's so important to get every part of you on the same page and on board with love! The only way to do this is to hear and validate all of your conflicting voices, and then let them know why it would actually be good for you to experience love. After all, every part of you loves you and wants you to succeed. Each part just has different ways of trying to achieve this.

1. Ask yourself: Is there any part(s) of me that doesn't want love right now or thinks it would somehow be bad for me to be/fall in love?

2. Listen compassionately to any love objections or hesitancies that come up. Try to understand how these parts are trying to help you or protect you from *perceived* danger. Keep in mind that it's impossible for you to be against yourself; this is simply your internal resistance presenting itself to you. Becoming aware of this resistance is helpful, because now you won't sabotage yourself in unconscious ways. Once you know your hesitancies, you can soothe, heal, and overcome them.

3. Open up a dialogue in your mind or on paper with each and every part of you that's not on board with love. Help them to see that by "protecting" you, they are actually hurting you and keeping you from getting what you all want—love! Here's how an inner dialogue might sound:

> **You:** Does any part of me think that love is a bad idea?
>
> **Your resistance:** Me! Remember the last time, when you got your heart smashed into a million pieces? Let's definitely not do *that* again.

You: I hear you. Thanks for looking out for me. I appreciate your care and concern. I love you for wanting to keep us safe, but I've got this. If we do get heartbroken again, I'll heal again. But I don't think that's going to happen, since now I realize what I want and what I need, so I'm in a much better position to pick a good match for me, for us! Let it be my job to worry. And if you're still scared, that's okay. I'll hold your hand through this whole process.

Your resistance: All right, if you say so! I'm still nervous, but if love would make you happy, then I'll try not to stop it.

You can repeat this process as often as necessary to lessen any resistance that arises and improve your relationship with all aspects of yourself!

Create a Love Vision Board

No matter what your ideal love life is, it will help the manifestation process to literally see it! In this exercise, you'll make a vision board specific to your love life. Have fun creating it, then use it every day as a reference for inspiration and motivation. The very acts of creating and admiring your vision board will support the energy of your desire.

If you're not into paper crafts, don't worry. You can do this online via a *Pinterest* board or digital collage. Also, this is a really fun and powerful activity to do in a group. Have your friends over to create vision boards and then take turns sharing key parts of each one. Here's how to make your love vision board:

1. Get a large piece of paper or poster board, glue, scissors, lots of magazines, and any other decorative scrapbooking items.
2. Cut out magazine pictures that represent the type of love you want to experience. You can also print out your own photos. Use images that make you think, *That's what I want!* They should capture the flavor of love you are looking for. While this might look like pictures of cute couples, it can also include words or images that describe how your relationship feels, sunsets you want to see together, activities you might do together, and so on.
3. Place the images and/or words onto your poster board in a fun and creative way that pleases your soul. Rearrange as needed, then glue or tape everything down securely.
4. Finally, hang up your board where you can be inspired by it often. If you don't have anywhere to hang it, tuck it away someplace safe, but take it out periodically to keep your desires in the front of your mind.

This visual reminder of your romantic goals will help keep your energy focused on what you want.

Write Authentic Affirmations to Attract Love

Repeating affirmations about your love life will help reprogram your mind to be open to a fulfilling relationship. In this exercise, you'll brainstorm uplifting statements to keep repeating to yourself (or to use in conversation with others) as you manifest love.

1. Get out a piece of paper or journal and list some positive, present-tense statements about your future love life. You can start with phrases like:
   * I am...
   * I am open to...
   * I am excited about...
   * My love is...
   * Our relationship is...
   * I feel...
2. Now you can write full affirmations based on these phrases. They can be things that are true now ("I'm excited to meet my match!") or things that will be true later ("We complement each other nicely and have similar values"). Here are some affirmations you might write:
   * My love life is about to get awesome.
   * I love my kind, supportive, and sexy partner.
   * We have so much fun creating a life together.
   * She/He/They love(s) how nerdy I am.
   * I am thankful for this beautiful relationship.

If only negative statements come to mind as you think about love, write those down first and then try to transform them from negatives to positives. You might turn "I suck at relationships" into "I'm practicing getting better at relating." Or turn "Love never works out for me" into "Just because it hasn't worked out in the past doesn't mean it can't now!"

Once you have your list of affirmations, get creative with how you use them. Meditate on them, affirm them in conversations, repeat them to yourself whenever you feel doubt, or recite them every morning or night as a part of your daily routine. Have fun with it!

Be Your Own Perfect Partner

If you want to manifest your soul mate, the fastest way to do it is to become your own soul mate first! Think of this activity as a game where you love and romance yourself so as to live as if your love wishes have already been fulfilled.

The game is simple: Think of how you want your future partner to treat you, and then go and do that for yourself. Don't do it because you are lacking a partner and you *have* to, but because you are your own best partner, first and foremost! Anything you can do to help yourself feel romanced or loved will do the trick. This activity is about living a mindset: If you were married to yourself, what would you do for yourself?

Here are some examples of how to do this, but get creative in however you want to practice it:

* Write yourself a love letter.
* Take yourself out to a nice dinner.
* Buy yourself some flowers of appreciation.
* Treat yourself to your favorite chocolates.
* Watch a romantic movie.
* Do something nice for your future self in anticipation of your needs. For example, set up what you need for your morning coffee or tea the night before.
* Draw a romantic bubble bath for yourself.
* Cook yourself a yummy meal.
* Remind yourself how good-looking you are.
* Ask yourself how you are doing throughout the day to take care of yourself emotionally.

Doing things like this regularly can help you cultivate feelings of love and romance in your life, which will point your energy in the right direction for manifesting an amazing partner.

Hydrate While Harmonizing with Love

A super easy way to attune to the energetic frequency of love is to literally ingest the energy of love into your body. In this exercise, you will program some drinking water (or other water-based drink of choice) with love and then drink it.

1. Choose your drink and pour it into your favorite glass. The more water it contains, the better. (It's best to avoid dehydrators like caffeine and alcohol.)
2. Hold the glass in both hands and imagine something or someone that you love very much, such as a person, a good memory, or a favorite place. For at least sixty seconds, concentrate on this feeling of love with pure positive focus. Now imagine yourself infusing your drink with this powerful energy. Picture this love energy literally changing and upgrading the composition of your drink. Water is energetically very impressionable, so you are upgrading its energetic makeup with your thoughts when you do this.
3. Drink up! As you hydrate, you are physically and spiritually harmonizing with love.

You already know that drinking water is good for your body. Why not use this exercise to make it good for your vibe as well?

Enlist a Crystal to Help You Manifest Love

Crystals can help with physical healing, de-stressing, promoting confidence, working through emotional blocks, and many other goals. For this exercise, you'll choose a crystal to help you manifest love.

1. Pick your "love crystal." Most pink, red, or green stones are associated with the heart chakra and therefore love, such as:
   * Rose Quartz: a gentle stone that represents the universal nature of love in all forms. It also encourages nurturing relationships, friendships, and emotional support.
   * Ruby: a more passionate stone that carries the frequencies of desire, sensuality, deep emotions, and true love.
   * Lapis Lazuli: a stone that supports your readiness to love and be loved.
2. Cleanse your crystal by rinsing it with running water (water straight from nature is best), smudging it (by burning your favorite cleansing plant near it), or burying it in the dirt temporarily. (Some crystals can't get wet, so double-check the best way to cleanse yours ahead of time.)
3. Hold the stone near your heart and mentally or verbally ask it to help you manifest love. If you're sensitive, you may even feel an energetic *yes* response from the stone. You can also meditate with the stone to establish a bond.
4. Charge your crystal by putting it out for a night in the moonlight during the full moon or in full sun during a sunny day.
5. Place your crystal in a part of your home that has to do with your love life (such as your bedroom, the relationship corner of your home as shown in feng shui, by your love vision board, etc.). You could also wear it as jewelry.

Using a crystal is a powerful (and beautiful!) way to promote feelings of love within and around you.

Make a Love Dream Jar

Many children write their secret wishes down and hide them away in a box or container. It's time to revisit that practice and make your own adult dream jar! In this exercise, you'll create a special place for your dreams about love to sit and marinate.

1. Purchase or find and decorate a small jar, box, or other container. Make sure it is small enough to tuck away somewhere safe (or, if you prefer, you can put it out on display). Keep some sticky notes or small pieces of paper in or near your jar.
2. Every time a new love desire enters your mind, write it down on one of your small pieces of paper, fold it up, and place it in your jar. As you do this, set the intention to "set it and forget it." Trust that the Universe is well acquainted with the contents of your jar, and as soon as you place something in it, the Universe gets to work on it.
3. After some time of collecting your love desires—you can wait weeks, months, or years, whatever feels right to you—revisit your jar and read what you once wanted. Take some time to notice and appreciate how many of your intentions came true, because they will!

In your next relationship, you can even share the wishes with your partner. You'll both be blown away by how much your relationship mirrors your original intentions.

Improve Your Love Frequency with Sound

All energy vibrates at a different frequency. Frequency hacking is a way to purposefully tune your energy to a certain frequency for the sake of becoming a better vibrational match to what you want. The closer a vibrational match you are to the frequency of love, the faster you will find it. In this manifesting practice, you'll use sound as a tool. There are two different ways you can do this: through healing frequencies or songs that light you up.

Love Frequencies

Get in a comfortable position, sitting or lying down, and use headphones to listen to your favorite healing frequencies, specifically ones that will tune you in to the frequency of love. Two of the best frequencies for love specifically are 528Hz and 639Hz. You can find many free ways to listen to these by searching online. Spend at least ten to twenty minutes breathing deeply as you let the harmonies alter your frequency.

Love Songs

Make a playlist of at least fifteen songs specifically designed to help yourself manifest love. Include any and all songs that make you feel in love, inspired by love, or excited to be in love. (Don't include any sad love songs, though, unless you want to be sad!) Listen to your playlist whenever it's convenient for you—such as on your way to work or while you're cleaning the house—to program your energy for love in the most easy and enjoyable way.

You can repeat either of these exercises daily or as often as you'd like!

Identify Your Love Preferences Through Contrast

With each "failed" attempt at love, we learn more about what works for us and what doesn't. In this exercise, you'll look at your past to get clarity on your love preferences so you can manifest a love that's truly in alignment with your values. These steps will walk you through how to discover what type of person or relationship is the best fit for you.

1. Make a two-column chart for every past lover/relationship you've had. Title each chart with the person's name. Title the left column "What Didn't Work" and the right column "What Worked."

2. In the left column for each chart, write down what didn't work for you in this relationship. Was the person mean, incompatible, sloppy, unsupportive? Was the relationship too fast, too consuming, too shallow, too rocky? In the right column, write down what you *did* like about this relationship. Was the person funny, romantic, great at planning dates? Was the relationship respectful, fun, passionate?

3. Once you've gone through every relationship and listed what worked and didn't work in each, review everything and see if you notice any patterns. Did certain personality traits or characteristics keep coming up, good or bad? Did certain types of relationships feel better to you than others?

4. Put this data to good use in your real life and start living in alignment with your preferences! Stop settling for traits that you already know don't work for you so you can keep space open for what does.

Observing trends and patterns is a powerful way to gain awareness about where you are now, where you want to be, and what to do differently to get there.

Challenge Your Negative Thoughts about Love

We all have some limiting beliefs about every topic in life. But when it comes to love, these limiting thoughts can be especially rampant since it can take several tries to land a good relationship. Use this exercise to rework some negativity and open yourself up to new possibilities. Remind yourself: Just because it didn't work out before doesn't mean it won't in the future!

1. Ask yourself: "What limiting or negative beliefs do I have about love, dating, relationships?" Then take some time to write down whatever comes to you (no matter how ridiculous it looks on paper). For example:
    *   Love is painful.
    *   Relationships are impossible for me.
    *   All men suck. There are no good men out there.
    *   What's the point? I'll probably just end up divorced like my parents.
    *   My ex was the only one for me.
    *   I'll never understand women. How can I be with one?
    *   Vulnerability is dangerous.
    *   The people I like never like me back.
2. Go down your list one by one and question what you've been believing up until this point by asking: "Can I know *for certain* that this is absolutely true/the only truth or possibility, or am I just biased or traumatized?" Even better, go down your list and argue the opposite perspective, which could be just as true, if not truer! Here's how that challenging might look:
    *   Can I know for certain that *all* men suck? Well...technically, they don't *all* suck. My dad is a good guy. My coworker Greg seems really nice. So there are at least two!

* Is it 100 percent true that vulnerability is always dangerous? It feels dangerous because it's scary for me, but vulnerability is actually the only way to create true intimacy and emotional safety in a relationship. How can true love happen without my being my true self? Being uncomfortable practicing vulnerability is a small price to pay for a loving relationship.
* Was my ex the *only* one for me? It feels like it, but I haven't met everyone in the world, so I can't be 100 percent certain. It's possible that there are more people like them, or even better for me than them! And if someone doesn't see my value and doesn't want to be with me, then they are definitely *not* the one for me!

All words are powerful—the ones we say aloud and the ones we think to ourselves. Rework the negative stories you've created so you can bolster your efforts with possibility and open-mindedness instead.

Use Self-Inquiry to Release Your Love Blockages

When it comes to love, there are many ways you may be unknowingly stopping yourself from fully being open. The good news is, this is usually just an innocent "protective" mechanism, rather than blatant self-sabotage. But if you're really ready for love, it's time to drop the walls and let love in! Here's how:

1. Find some quiet time and set the intention to get genuinely curious. Take a few moments to release any judgment of yourself and replace it with wanting to understand yourself so as to discover empowering information that will help your love life.
2. Meditate or journal on the following questions:
   * What's been holding me back from experiencing the kind of love I want?
   * What can I do differently this time to get a different result?
   * What feelings am I trying to experience from love and what's stopping me from feeling that way now?
   * What needs am I trying to get met through a partner, and how can I get them met in other ways for now (either through myself or others)?
   * What am I afraid of when it comes to love? How can I go toward love and create an internal safety net at the same time?
   * What am I willing to do, change, or accept in order to becoming more loving toward myself and others?

These questions can feel uncomfortable to ponder at first. But the deeper you go into self-reflection, the closer you get to finding a relationship that's truly right for you.

CHAPTER 3

MANIFESTING FINANCIAL ABUNDANCE

Whether your finances are lacking and you crave the safety and security of having enough, or your bank account is healthy but you're curious to see just how much wealth you can create, manifesting more money is never a bad idea. Either way, this chapter will help you get there, one exercise at a time!

As you manifest more money, keep in mind that:

* It is not necessarily selfish or materialistic to want money. Money is just a helpful resource.
* Money is simply a form of energy. Help your energy flow and you will help your money flow.
* More money is being created all the time. You having more doesn't mean someone else has to have less.
* Money isn't good or evil; it is what you make of it!

Let's get started. Financial freedom is calling!

Discover What You Really Want Financially

How do you think more money will make your life *feel* better? In this exercise, you'll answer this important personal question so you can realize and pursue your true values. It's important to discover your true values because money desires are always deeper than the money itself!

1. Ask yourself *why* you want to manifest financial abundance. Hint: It always comes down to how you want to *feel*. For example, you may think, *I want to manifest financial abundance so I can feel like a good provider, relaxed, blessed, free to travel, able to quit my job...*

2. Focus your thoughts, feelings, decisions, actions, and life in a way that helps you cultivate the feelings you want to experience in your financial reality right now. To assist you with this, ask yourself these two questions and write down whatever comes to you:
   * What's stopping me from feeling how I want to feel right now?
   * How can I feel more the way I want to feel until the money comes?

3. Use your discoveries from steps one and two to make empowering adjustments to your daily life so that you can start feeling more of how you want to feel today! For example, perhaps you can feel like a good provider now by anticipating the needs of the people around you. Maybe you can make a point to feel more relaxed by spending more time in nature.

When you figure out how to feel blessed now, you'll manifest many more blessings.

Claim Your Abundance via Journaling

This exercise will help you recognize and really *feel* the blessings in your life so as to manifest more of them. Add this journal practice to your morning routine, and your life will upgrade faster than you can imagine!

Here are a few pointers before you begin your journal entry:

* Write in the *present tense,* as if your dream reality were already a fact.
* Use *specifics* to make it feel more real to you (but don't limit the amount of money you want by putting a number on it; instead, say, "I would like this *or* something better/more").
* Emphasize how you are *feeling* in this future reality.
* Use a real pen/pencil and paper to write the entry by hand.
* Don't limit the Universe by planning exactly *how* and *when* this will all come about.

As you journal, imagine your ideal financial outcome and write down what it will be like, as if it were already your reality. Use some of these phrases to get things started:

* I am grateful for...
* I am already abundant because...
* I'm thankful that...
* I appreciate _____ in my life.
* Being financially abundant makes me feel...
* My relationship to money is...
* I love being able to...
* I spend my money doing, buying, investing...

Think of this written visualization as the combination of a gratitude entry for what you have now and a daydreaming session about your financial future!

Meditate to Become One with Money

Though it's easy to fall into the trap of feeling like money is a finite resource, it's actually just as abundant as anything else in the Universe. This meditation is designed to help you reconnect to your natural flow of abundance in the form of financial prosperity. Follow these steps:

1. Sit or lie down comfortably. Close your eyes, lengthen your spine, uncross your limbs, and turn your palms up.
2. Set the intention to become a conduit for money and channel for wealth.
3. Focus on slowing down your breath. With each inhale and exhale, feel your body expand and contract (as if your entire body were one big lung). Continue this breathing and opening your body for a few minutes.
4. Now think of an image that represents money to you (dollars, yen, rupees, etc.). See this image appear above your head and then flow down into your body, becoming a part of you. The money fills the space in your brain, then your neck and shoulders, arms and torso, hips, legs, feet, and so on. Breathe more money in with each breath. Continue visualizing this money being absorbed into you until you become so full of money that you have to release some of it to make space for more. Breathe in money, breathe out money. Let it flow as you become the ultimate channel of this energy.
5. Stay in this flow for as long as it feels good, noticing how the money supply never ends.

This meditation will help you embody financial abundance and eventually manifest more.

Create a Money Vision Board

Chances are, if you want to manifest more money, you've already thought about all the amazing things you would do with it. Now it's time to put those ideas into pictures and make your money vision board.

If you're not into paper crafts, don't worry. You can do this online via a *Pinterest* board or digital collage. Also, this is a really fun and powerful activity to do in a group. Have your friends over to create vision boards and then take turns sharing key parts of each one. Here's how to make your financial vision board:

1. Get out a large piece of paper or poster board, glue, scissors, lots of magazines, and any other decorative scrapbooking items.

2. Cut out magazine pictures that represent the type of lifestyle you want to experience. You can also print out your own photos. Use images that make you think, *That's what I want!* They should capture the flavor of abundance you are looking for. For example, you might cut out pictures of your dream home, dream car, ideal vacation scenarios, and so on. You cannot be too outrageous or too materialistic in this exercise, so suspend any self-judgment or thoughts of lack for a few hours, and just have fun.

3. Place the images and/or words onto your poster board in a fun and creative way that pleases your soul. Rearrange as needed, then glue or tape everything down securely.

4. Finally, hang up your board where you can be inspired by it often. If you don't have anywhere to hang it, tuck it away someplace safe, but take it out periodically to keep your desires in the front of your mind.

This visual reminder of your financial goals will help keep your energy focused on what you want.

Write Affirmations That Support Financial Abundance

Self-talk matters, especially when it comes to your financial confidence. In this exercise, you'll create some beneficial perspectives to help you reconnect to your abundance abilities.

1. Get out a piece of paper or journal and list some positive, present-tense statements about your future financial situation. You can start with phrases like:
   * I am…
   * I am open to…
   * I am excited about…
   * My finances are…
   * My relationship to money is…
   * I feel…
2. Now you can write full affirmations based on these phrases. They can be things that are true now ("I'm getting better with my finances every day") or things that will be true when you are experiencing your desired financial abundance ("I can buy whatever I want, whenever I want!"). Here are some affirmations you might write:
   * I'm getting my finances more organized than ever before.
   * I love making money!
   * My life is very abundant.
   * I'm transitioning from working for my money to my money working for me!
   * I am ready to receive more money than I have in the past.
   * I'm excited to experience how abundant I can be.

Authenticity is key here. If a statement feels fake or fraudulent, soften it to make it feel more true and empowering for you. For example, "I'm a millionaire!" can feel untrue if you're not there yet. Soften it by changing it to, "I'm on my way to becoming a millionaire," "I'm open to making more money than I have before," or "I'm ready to learn how to create wealth for myself." Same idea, different wording!

Once you have your list of affirmations, get creative with how you use them. Meditate on them, affirm them in conversations, repeat them to yourself whenever you feel doubt, or recite them every morning or night as a part of your daily routine. Have fun with it!

Live in Harmony with Your Financial Wishes

The easiest way to manifest more financial abundance is to start feeling more abundant in general. This exercise will help you come up with plenty of ways to do just that. First, there are two questions to consider:

1. What do you do, say, or think that makes you feel *less* abundant? Doing less of this will help you feel more abundant.
2. What can you do, say, or think that would help you feel *more* abundant? Do more of this to increase feelings of abundance.

Here are a few ideas for building feelings of abundance:

* Start a daily gratitude journal.
* Take inventory of everything you do have (as opposed to what you don't have yet).
* Give service providers big tips when and because you can.
* Instead of trying to save money (which can happen from thoughts of lack), challenge yourself to make more money (this encourages thoughts of expansion).
* Donate to charity to spread the wealth.
* Keep money all around your home to remind you that money is everywhere.
* Start investing, even if it's in small amounts.
* Cook a big, healthy meal that will produce lots of extra food and leftovers.
* Be of service to others.

As you can see, these ideas don't all have to revolve around money. Any feelings of abundance will improve your financial life!

Program Your Drinking Water to Promote Abundance

It's time to turn your boring drinking water into a magical abundance elixir! Water is a vitally important natural resource—you need it to live, and your body is made up mostly of water. It can also hold an energetic charge, so you can program your water for success, then keep yourself hydrated with water that's filled with your intentions.

1. Choose your drink and pour it into your favorite glass. The more water it contains, the better. (It's best to avoid dehydrators like caffeine and alcohol.) For extra credit you can choose a glass that represents abundance to you. Maybe it's shiny and gold or green like money!
2. Hold the glass in both hands and imagine something that symbolizes money, wealth, or prosperity to you. That could be dollar signs, coins, or an image of all the things your future money will buy. For at least sixty seconds, concentrate on these images. Imagine yourself infusing your drink with this powerful energy.
3. Drink up! As you hydrate, you are physically and spiritually harmonizing with success and financial abundance while raising the frequency of your body's energy.

As you take in this drink charged with prosperity, your body's energy will rise to match the high frequency of abundance. You're now more of a match to what you want than you were a few minutes ago.

Activate a Crystal to Encourage Prosperity

What better way to manifest additional precious and valuable resources than with precious and valuable stones? Plus, since "like attracts like," shiny things can help attract more shiny things. So let crystals help you to get that coin!

1. Pick your "money crystal." Anything green or gold, like money, is best! For example, you can use:
   * Pyrite (a.k.a. fool's gold): an amazing money manifestation stone that increases confidence and draws in opportunity.
   * Citrine: a yellowish-brown stone that helps to energize you and your finances.
   * Malachite: a beautiful dark-green stone that helps you release blockages and create positive change.
2. Cleanse your crystal by rinsing it with running water (water straight from nature is best), smudging it (by burning your favorite cleansing plant near it), or burying it in the dirt temporarily. (Some crystals can't get wet, so double-check the best way to cleanse yours ahead of time.)
3. Hold the stone to your heart and mentally or verbally ask it to help you manifest financial abundance. If you're sensitive, you may feel an energetic *yes* response from the stone. You can also meditate with the stone to establish a bond.
4. Charge your crystal by putting it out for a night in the moonlight during the full moon or in full sun during a sunny day.
5. Place your crystal in a part of your home that has to do with your prosperity (like your office or desk, the prosperity corner of your home as described by feng shui, by your financial vision board, etc.). You could also wear it as jewelry.

Crystals are a powerful (and beautiful!) way to promote feelings of financial abundance within and around you.

Use Sight and Sound to Become an
Energetic Match to Financial Abundance

Did you know you can use sight and sound as tools to help you manifest financial abundance? Here's how.

Sight: Abundance Imagery

Find an image, video, symbol, sigil, or frequency depiction of abundance, financial freedom, prosperity, or wealth. Maybe it's an image of an abundant field of crops. Maybe it's a treasure chest overflowing with golden coins. Maybe it's an energy grid that represents abundance. Pick whatever you like!

For at least eleven minutes, gently gaze at this image in a relaxed and meditative way. This will give you enough time to really begin to attune to the vibration of the imagery. As you focus, imagine becoming one with the image. Let it into your psyche so you can sync up with it.

Sound: Abundance Frequencies

Get in a comfortable position, sitting or lying down, and use headphones to listen to your favorite healing frequencies, specifically ones that will tune you in to abundance. One of the best frequencies for abundance specifically is 888Hz. You can find many free ways to listen to this frequency by searching online. Spend at least ten to twenty minutes breathing deeply as you let the harmonies alter your frequency.

Wealth Playlist

Make a playlist of at least eight songs designed to help yourself manifest money. (We'll use the number 8 because this number carries the frequency of abundance and infinity.) Include any and all songs that make you feel abundant, rich, and successful. Listen to your playlist whenever you feel inspired to.

Repeat either of these exercises daily or as often as you'd like!

Take Time to Daydream

Daydreaming isn't a waste of time—it's a stepping-stone to bigger and better things! In this exercise, please allow your imagination to run wild.

1. Every day for ten days, imagine that life just handed you an extra lump sum of money. For the first day, choose a small amount, like $100, $500, or $1,000. Then make a list of all the things you would enjoy spending it on. You have to use up every imaginary dollar.
2. The next day, imagine that you received ten times the amount of pretend money you had yesterday, and spend all this new money in your mind. What would you get or do? How would you allocate it? How many experiences can you create with it?
3. The next day, imagine that you got one hundred times yesterday's amount of money. Make a list of new things you will use up all of your money on. Keep repeating this imaginary spending spree for at least ten days, increasing the amount of money exponentially each day.

After a while, you may discover that it gets difficult to think of new ways to use that much money. That's okay; keep stretching your mind and opening yourself to new possibilities. Even though it will just feel like a fun thing to do, every time you play this game you're actually priming yourself to receive financial abundance!

Turn Lack Into Abundance

In this exercise, you'll transform a "lack" mentality into one of abundance, one thought, word, and action at a time. A perception of scarcity will always make you a match to a lack of abundance. In order to change the experience, you must first change your attitude. These tips will help:

1. Start noticing when you participate in thoughts, speech, or actions that are sponsored by a scarcity or lack mindset. For example, you may take a job you hate just because you need the money, believing there aren't enough good opportunities out there. Or you may hoard money instead of letting it flow. Or you may often think things like, *I can't afford that*. Do not criticize yourself when you notice these things; just observe them in order to make yourself aware of what you are doing.

2. Then get curious and ask questions, such as:
   * Where did I learn this thought or action?
   * Is it actually my truth, or is it something that I picked up along my journey?
   * Do I still want to keep holding on to it, or would I rather believe/do something that feels better to me?

3. Lastly, use your imagination to move yourself into a more abundant mindset, whether for your life in general or for a specific situation. To do that, ask yourself questions like:
   * What would I do if I knew there were plenty more opportunities on the way?
   * How would I handle my money if I knew that more would always come around?
   * What would I do in my current situation if I had all the money in the world?

Even if abundance does not feel like your current reality, asking questions like these will help open your mind to a more abundant way of living.

Practice this self-awareness technique daily to make a mindset of abundance the new standard for yourself.

Identify Your Self-Limiting Beliefs about Money

Your programming around money will always dictate how much you let it in. Common sayings like "Money is the root of all evil" and "Money doesn't grow on trees" brainwash us into thinking small by making money essentially bad, and implying that we will hardly ever have enough of it. The good news is, you get to reprogram yourself, starting now! This exercise can help you reframe your thinking about money:

1. Identify any limiting or negative beliefs you have about money, finances, and financial freedom. Most of these beliefs probably came from your family, your friends, the media, and society. They may include sentiments like:
   * You have to work hard to make money.
   * One person having more means other people have less.
   * All rich people are terrible.
   * More money, more problems.
   * If I have a lot of money, people will only pretend to like me so they can take advantage of me.
   * Money is a superficial thing to want.
2. Go down your list one by one and question what you've been believing by asking: Can I know *for certain* that this is absolutely true/the only truth or possibility (or am I just biased/programmed)? Even better, go down your list and argue the opposite perspective, which could be just as true, if not truer! Here are some examples of how that conversation might go:
   * Is it really true that all rich people are bad people? No, there are also some great rich people out there who use their wealth for good, and I would like to be one of those. Besides, there are plenty of poor people who are terrible

too, so maybe it's less about the money and more about the individual.

* Is it 100 percent true that if I make more money, I'll have more problems? Maybe I'll have some *different* problems, but maybe I'll have fewer problems because I can use the money to pay for support in different areas of my life. I could afford a nanny, a great tax accountant, a personal chef, a personal assistant—this would actually make my life much easier!

* Is money really a superficial thing to want? Money is just a tool that we use and an important part of the way our society works. It's not superficial to want to be more resourced. It's smart!

Identifying and questioning your beliefs can help you shift your mindset. And no, money doesn't *directly* grow on trees. But the paper used to create money does. So...maybe money kind of does grow on trees after all!

Replace Your Old Money Habits

When it comes to manifesting money, it's all about the energy of flux and flow (inflow of money and outflow of money) and an attitude of abundance (there is always more where that came from). Money energy doesn't like being restricted—it's best to let it roll in and out like the tide. Sometimes we don't realize how we subconsciously sabotage our money-manifesting efforts by participating in old, restrictive, habits that no longer serve us. In this exercise, you'll discover what some of those habits might be and how you can replace them with some new, more empowering ones! Here's how:

1. Find some quiet time to yourself and set an intention to get genuinely curious. Take a few moments to release any judgment of yourself or your life and replace it with a desire to understand yourself and your life in order to discover empowering information that will help your financial situation.

2. Meditate or journal on the following questions:
   * What's been holding me back from experiencing the kind of financial freedom I want?
   * What can I do differently to improve my circumstances?
   * What needs am I trying to meet through financial freedom, and how can I meet them in other ways for now?
   * What am I afraid of when it comes to becoming wealthier? How can I still go toward wealth and create internal safety at the same time?
   * What am I willing to do, change, or accept in order to feel more abundant about my life in general?

These questions can help you overcome resistance and manifest your financial desires.

Get All Your Rowers Working Together

Imagine a rowboat with six people rowing it. If three are rowing in one direction and three are rowing in another, the boat will never make any progress. But if all the rowers work toward a common goal, they can achieve great things! That's what you'll be doing in this exercise—getting all your internal rowers rowing in the direction of more money. Here's what to do:

1. Ask yourself: "Is there any part(s) of me that doesn't want more money/financial freedom right now or thinks it would somehow be bad for me to have it?" For example, a part of you might believe that if you have more money, people will use you or take advantage of you. Another part of you might hate taxes enough to secretly stop you from manifesting more money just so you don't have to pay more in taxes!

2. Listen compassionately to any objections or hesitancies that come up within you. See how these objecting parts of you actually are just trying to help you because they see more money as potentially dangerous or threatening. Whatever comes up is your internal resistance presenting itself to you. Becoming aware of this is so helpful, because now you don't have to sabotage yourself anymore. Once you know your hesitancies, you can soothe, heal, and overcome them.

3. Open up a dialogue in your mind or on paper with each and every part of you that's not on board the money boat. Help them to see that by "protecting" you, they are actually hurting you and keeping you from getting what you want—more wealth! Here's what that dialogue might sound like:

   You: Does any part of me think that having more money is a bad idea?

Your resistance: Me! You don't want to end up like your dad, marrying women who only want to be with you for your money.

You: I understand that concern. I don't want that either, but just because that happened to him doesn't mean it will happen to me. I have plenty of great qualities that women like about me that have nothing to do with money. That's not going to change once I have more.

Your resistance: Okay, that makes sense. I feel a little better now.

You can repeat this exercise as often as necessary.

CHAPTER 4

MANIFESTING VIBRANT HEALTH

Health is your body's desired state of being, but sometimes we all need a little help reclaiming physical harmony. Maybe you want a speedy recovery from an injury or illness, or maybe you're ready to raise your energy levels to better embrace your best life. No matter what your current health status, there's always room for improvement, and you can use manifestation and the Law of Attraction to help!

As you manifest your improved state of health, remember that:

* Dis-ease is just that—when you're not at ease and harmony is not happening at an optimal level in the body or mind. Create more harmony and you'll experience more ease. Your body knows what to do from there!
* If you're feeling unwell, it's usually because a part of you is trying to send you a helpful message (to slow down, eat better, think differently, etc.).
* Temporarily living in a state that makes you unhappy (like unhealthiness) can always lead to expansion (better health)!
* Self-love is a really effective cure-all.
* Anything is possible! Miracles happen all the time.

Let's dive into some exercises and activities that can help you recharge, rebalance, and restore your health. Your most healthy self is calling!

Name Your Deepest Health Desires

Everyone has different intentions for their health. For some, more energy and a better memory would be nice. For someone who is ill, simply the absence of dis-ease would be amazing. Whatever your body needs, you can manifest—especially once you understand the core feelings you want to experience as a result of being healthier. Follow these steps to discover what you would like your physical being to feel like:

1. Ask yourself why you want to manifest better health/your ideal health goal. For example, you might say, *I want to improve my mental health so I can live free of anxiety and depression and enjoy my life more.*

2. Focus your thoughts, feelings, decisions, actions, and life in a way that helps you to cultivate the feelings you want to experience in your future health goals. To assist you, ask yourself these questions and write down whatever comes to you:

   * What's stopping me from feeling how I want to feel right now?

     To answer this question, you might write something like, *I haven't reached out for help with my mental health. I haven't changed my diet at all. I'm not exercising regularly. I'm not sleeping well. I hate everything about my job. I don't have any friends or family in town.*

   * How can I feel more of how I want to feel at this moment? How can I feel more like I'm living my best life and enjoying my time?

     As a response, you might write, *I could change jobs. I could move closer to friends and family. I could make some new connections here. I could take that trip I've always wanted to take.*

3. Use your discoveries from steps one and two to make empowering adjustments to your daily life so that you can feel more of how you want to feel today! Put some of your ideas from step two into action. Release any resistance you've identified in the process.

List Your Top Health Priorities

Because we are such complex beings, we have many areas of health and wellness to tend to. Physical, mental, emotional, and spiritual health/wellness are all equally important and work together to support our overall vitality. Improve one area, and all the others improve as well! In this exercise, you'll look at each area and write down phrases or scenarios of how your perfect health would look so as to call it into reality.

Here are a few pointers before you begin your exercise:

* Write in the *present tense,* as if your dream reality were already a fact.
* Use *specifics* to make it feel more real to you.
* Emphasize how you are *feeling* in this future reality.
* Use a real pen/pencil and paper to write the entry by hand (no typing!).
* Don't limit the Universe by planning exactly *how* and *when* this will all come about.

Get at least four pieces of paper to write on, one for each area of health. Label the top of each with one area of health (e.g., Physical, Mental, Emotional, Spiritual) and write out what you wish to manifest in that area. Here are some prompts you can use to help you:

* I feel _____ in my body/mind/emotions/spirit.
* I love being able to...
* I'm thankful for...
* I'm happy that I can...
* I enjoy...
* I (insert healthy daily habit here)...
* I no longer need to (insert old health-inhibiting habit here)...

Repeat those prompts for each area of health until you've covered them all.

This exercise can help you feel grateful for the health and wellness you do have while also manifesting your ideal health.

Bask in Healing Light via Meditation

Health is the state of harmony that you experience in the absence of dis-ease. Embrace more ease, and you'll improve your health! In this meditation you'll sit back, relax, and let a bright, cleansing, and healing light come over you and wash away any dis-ease, making space for healing. Follow these steps:

1. Sit or lie down comfortably. Close your eyes, lengthen your spine, uncross your limbs, and turn your palms up.
2. Set the intention to let go and trust your innate intelligence to heal any health problems or improve whatever dis-ease you may currently be experiencing.
3. For several minutes, take slow, deep breaths, and imagine yourself in a beautiful, relaxing, safe place. This could be a field of flowers, a forest, a fluffy cloud—whatever feels relaxing and rejuvenating to you. What does this healing place look like? What sounds can you hear? What's the overall vibe? Be present with this place as you let yourself unwind.
4. Now imagine that from above, a warm light twinkles and expands downward toward you. See this light coming closer; you feel that it is good and helpful. Ask the light to heal and cleanse you. Let the light come over your body slowly, like honey, starting at your head and dripping down to your toes. Everything the light touches becomes soothed and healed. This magical healing energy cures all. Soak in this light bath for as long as it feels good!

Do this meditation whenever you want to feel cleansed and refreshed so as to support your overall well-being.

Create a Wellness Vision Board

The optimal image of health may only exist in your mind right now, but as soon as you put it on paper, it's only a matter of time until it becomes a physical reality as well. Assembling a representation of your optimal health in the form of a vision board can inspire and guide you every day.

If you're not into paper crafts, don't worry. You can do this online via a *Pinterest* board or digital collage. Also, this is a really fun and powerful activity to do in a group. Have your friends over to create vision boards and then take turns sharing key parts of each one. Here's how to make your wellness vision board:

1. Get a large piece of paper or poster board, glue, scissors, lots of magazines, and any other decorative scrapbooking items.
2. Cut out magazine pictures that represent the type of healthy lifestyle you want to experience. You can also print out your own photos. Use images that make you think, *That's what I want!* They should capture the flavor of health and vitality you are looking for. For example, you might cut out pictures of your favorite health foods and recipes, relaxing images that soothe your nervous system, pictures of you smiling, words and phrases related to your best health, and so on.
3. Place the images and/or words onto your poster board in a fun and creative way that pleases your soul. Rearrange as needed, then glue or tape everything down securely.
4. Finally, hang up your board where you can be inspired by it often. If you don't have anywhere to hang it, tuck it away someplace safe, but take it out periodically to keep your desires in the front of your mind.

This visual reminder of your health goals will keep you focused and motivated on your journey to wellness.

Recite Well-Being Affirmations

Words are incredibly powerful. When you tell yourself that you are well or can get better, your body will listen. Writing affirmations that promote inner and outer wellness can help you manifest these goals.

1. Get out a piece of paper or journal and list some positive, present-tense statements about your desired health. You can start with phrases like:
    *   I am...
    *   I am open to...
    *   I am excited about...
    *   My health is...
    *   My relationship to my body/mind/soul is...
    *   I feel...

2. Now you can write full affirmations based on these phrases. They can be things that are true now ("My relationship with food is healing more every day") or things that will be true later ("I feel young again!"). Here are some affirmations you might write:
    *   I am full of energy and get through my day easily.
    *   I love eating well and nourishing my body with yummy things.
    *   My health is improving thanks to my morning routine.
    *   I feel grateful to be free of dis-ease and pain.
    *   I am excited to experience how good I can really feel.
    *   I'm dedicated to adopting a new health habit every month!

Don't forget, you can always tweak an affirmation that doesn't feel authentic to you at the moment. For example, "I'm super healthy!" may feel untrue if you're not there yet. Soften it by changing it to "I'm on my way to better health" or "Improved health is possible for me."

This new wording can help you transition from where you are now to where you want to be.

Once you have your list of affirmations, get creative with how you use them. Meditate on them, affirm them in conversations, repeat them to yourself whenever you feel doubt, or recite them every morning or night as a part of your daily routine. Have fun with it!

Live As If You Were at Peak Health

This exercise is like a game in which you live as if your health wishes have already been fulfilled (to the degree that you can). Think of how you would act and feel and what you would do if you were already your healthiest self and then do as much of that as you can today!

Here are some examples of how you can do this, but get creative in however you practice it:

* Treat yourself to some green juice as an afternoon snack.
* Join a gym or yoga studio.
* Invest in organic groceries out of respect for your body.
* Treat yourself to some vitamin D and relax by a body of water.
* Do something meditative that takes your mind off of everything stressful and brings you into your body (such as poetry, tai chi, fishing, dancing—whatever!).
* Do something nice for your future self in anticipation of your needs. For example, premake healthy snacks to take to work all week.
* Remind yourself how well your body/mind do already function.

As you begin practicing these things, ask yourself how you are doing throughout the day to take care of the needs of your body, mind, and soul. Adjust as needed.

Sip Healing Health Tonics

It's no secret that overall health has a lot to do with what you put in your body. Yes, it's great to support your health with nourishing foods and liquids, but have you ever tried charging them with healing energy before you consumed them? This is next-level health!

1. Choose your drink and pour it into your favorite glass. The more water it contains, the better. (It's best to avoid dehydrators like caffeine and alcohol.)
2. Hold the glass in both hands and imagine charging the drink with health, healing, white light, good vibes—whatever you feel your body needs in that moment. Picture this healing energy changing and upgrading the composition of the drink. You can also thank it in advance for all the nourishment it's about to provide your body.
3. Drink up! As you hydrate, you are physically and spiritually harmonizing with health and raising the frequency of your body simultaneously.

As you take in this drink charged with the intention of healing, your body will have to heal its energy to some degree in order to match this higher frequency. Repeat at every meal or whenever you feel inspired to!

Enlist Crystals to Encourage Perfect Health

Crystals' high frequency can help to raise your vibration and bring harmony to your mind and body. For this exercise, you'll choose a crystal to help you manifest good health.

1. Pick your "health crystal." Here are some of the best overall healing crystals:
   * Lepidolite: a soothing stone that helps calm the nervous system to allow for natural healing to take place.
   * Clear Quartz: sometimes referred to as the "master healer" because it helps align your energy and amplifies whatever intentions you set.
   * Selenite: a cleansing stone that can purify and reboot your system.
2. Cleanse your crystal by rinsing it with running water (water straight from nature is best), smudging it (by burning your favorite cleansing plant near it), or burying it in the dirt temporarily. (Some crystals can't get wet, so double-check the best way to cleanse yours ahead of time.)
3. Hold the stone to your heart and mentally or verbally ask it to help you manifest whatever your health goal is. If you're sensitive, you may feel an energetic *yes* response from the stone. You can also meditate with the stone to establish a bond.
4. Charge your crystal by putting it out for a night in the moonlight during the full moon or in full sun during a sunny day.
5. Place your crystal under your pillow or next to your bed so it can help you while you sleep, wear it as jewelry, or place it on any chakra while you lie down in meditation.

The strong natural energies of crystals can partner with you on your journey to improved health!

Preserve Your Health Intentions in a Jar

A dream jar or wish box is a powerful place to store your intentions while you trust that the Universe will help make them happen. Since you're manifesting improved health now, you can create a jar or container dedicated specifically to your health desires.

1. Purchase or find and decorate a small jar, box, or other container. Make sure it is small enough to tuck away somewhere safe (or, if you prefer, you can put it out on display). Because the feng shui area of the home related to health is in the center of the home (or the center of any room), it's best to store your dream jar there. Keep some sticky notes or small pieces of paper in or near your jar.

2. Every time a new health desire enters your mind, write it down on one of your small pieces of paper, fold it up, and place it in your jar. As you do this, set the intention to "set it and forget it." Trust that the Universe is well acquainted with the contents of your jar, and as soon as you place something in it, the Universe gets to work on it.

3. After some time of collecting your health desires—you can wait weeks, months, or years, whatever feels right to you— revisit your jar and read what you once wanted. Take some time to notice and appreciate how many of your intentions came true, because they will!

Writing down what you want and keeping those wishes in a dedicated space gives your intentions energetic weight and charge.

Use Sound to Improve Your Health

Like all other states of being, health is a *frequency*. The higher your energetic frequency, the healthier you are. Because of this, you can use certain frequencies, especially sound waves, to influence and upgrade your whole system! Try these methods:

Healing Frequencies

Get in a comfortable position, sitting or lying down, and use headphones to listen to your favorite healing frequencies, specifically ones that will attune you to health and healing. Some of the best frequencies for health and healing are 396Hz (for releasing fear) and 963Hz. You can find many free ways to listen to these by searching online. Spend at least ten to twenty minutes breathing deeply as you let the harmonies alter your frequency.

Songs

Make a playlist of at least six songs specifically designed to help yourself manifest your health goal. You'll chose six songs because the number 6 carries the frequency of improvement, harmony, and stability. Include any and all songs that make you feel healthy, happy, and peaceful. (Hint: The cells of the human body really love classical music for promoting healing!) Listen to your playlist every day first thing in the morning or the last thing before you go to sleep.

You can repeat either of these exercises daily or as often as you'd like.

Transform Sickness Into Health via Contrast

In life, it's contrast that leads to expansion, and your health is no exception. Every time you feel sick or unwell, you (consciously or subconsciously) ask for wellness in a more powerful way than ever before. In this exercise, you'll use the contrasting experiences of your health to help you gain clarity and momentum for what you'll manifest next. Here's how:

1. Make a quick inventory of any areas of your health that are suffering or could use support. Remember, these areas may be physical, mental, emotional, or spiritual. These dis-eases or pain points are the contrast that is causing you to birth new desires for better health.

2. Use your list as a starting point to clarify what you do want to create. For every item on your list, ask yourself, What would I rather be experiencing? Once you've identified what that is (hint: It's usually the opposite of whatever you are currently experiencing), cross off the original problem and replace it with the new desire. For example:
   * "Constant daily stress" gets crossed off and becomes "An overall sense of ease"
   * "Sleeplessness" becomes "Well rested and ready to go"
   * "Dependent on substances" becomes "Self-regulating in healthy ways"

3. By making this list, you have declared to the Universe what you no longer want to participate in, and you've defined exactly what you'd like to replace it with. Use this new information to alter your thoughts, habits, decisions, and actions to support your new creations.

Identifying contrast points is a powerful way to gain awareness about how you feel now and how you want to feel in order to make that your new reality.

Untangle Your Health Limitations

It's totally natural to entertain limiting thoughts for so long that they graduate into limiting beliefs. Use this exercise to rework some of your preprogrammed negativity and open yourself up to new possibilities for your health. Think outside of the box and let the old beliefs that are no longer serving you fade away (or at least become less prevalent). Follow these steps:

1. Ask yourself: "What limiting or negative beliefs do I have about my health and well-being?" Write down whatever comes to you (no matter how ridiculous it looks on paper). For example:
   * It's hard to be healthy.
   * I'll never heal my eczema.
   * What's the point of diet and exercise? I always gain the weight back later.
   * Because my parents had anxiety, I'm sure to have it too.
   * No doctor can figure out what's wrong with me.
2. Go down your list one by one and question what you've been believing up until this point by asking: Can I know *for certain* that this is absolutely true/the only truth or possibility (or am I just biased)? Even better, go down your list and argue the opposite perspective, which could be just as true, if not truer! Here's what that might look like:
   * Is it really hard to be healthy? It has been a challenge for me in the past, but I do enjoy some healthy foods, and it feels good to exercise once I've done it for several weeks in a row. So it's possible that being healthy isn't all *that* hard. Maybe it's harder to be unhealthy because that leads to so many problems!
   * Can I know for sure that my eczema will never go away? Well...no. I'm not a fortune-teller. And I've seen case studies

of people who have gotten rid of theirs, so it must be possible.

* No doctor has been able to figure out what's wrong with me...yet! Just because we don't have all the answers yet doesn't mean they can't or won't come.

When it comes to your health, negative self-talk is likely to worsen disease and exacerbate anything bothering you. Working together with your healthcare providers and undoing these self-limiting beliefs can bring significant improvements to your health.

Release Blockages to Manifesting Your Health

Health and harmony go hand in hand! When your body is in harmony, you feel healthy, but when you're out of balance, you experience dis-ease and health issues. Of course, this is never your fault or your doing, but if you can take responsibility to choose new and empowering ways to reclaim your harmony, you'll notice your health regenerate and/or improve itself!

1. Find some quiet time to yourself and set the intention to get genuinely curious. Take a few moments to release any judgment of yourself or your life and replace it with wanting to understand yourself and your life.
2. Meditate or journal on the following questions:
   * What's been holding me back from experiencing the kind of health, energy, and vitality I want?
   * What can I try differently to improve my overall well-being?
   * What feelings of ultimate health do I want to experience, and what's stopping me from feeling those ways now?
   * What needs am I trying to meet through obtaining perfect health, and how can I meet them in other creative ways for now?
   * What am I afraid of when it comes to becoming healthier? How can I still go toward health and create internal safety at the same time?
   * What am I willing to do, change, or accept in order to feel healthier/healed in general?

Answering questions like these can help you discover empowering information that will improve your health and well-being starting today.

Enlist Your Body's Collaboration and Cooperation for Your Good Health

Ironically, it's possible that certain parts of you believe the only way to get your health needs met is to make you *unhealthy* first. It might sound strange that some part of you might want to stay injured or sick, because every part of you is always on your side. But sometimes, certain types of dis-ease and health issues can serve to bring your attention back to slowing down and taking care of yourself. How do you deal with this situation? Get to know these parts of you, see what they want and need, and notice how they are ultimately intending to help you! Here's how:

1. Ask yourself: "Is there any part(s) of me that doesn't want to get better now or thinks it would somehow be bad for me to be in perfect health?"

2. Listen compassionately to any objections or hesitancies that come up. Try to understand how these parts are trying to help you or protect you from *perceived* danger. Keep in mind that it's impossible for you to be against yourself. Every part of you is trying to help, even if you can't see how yet. Becoming aware of this is so helpful, because now you don't have to sabotage yourself anymore. Once you know your hesitancies, you can soothe, heal, and overcome them.

3. Open up a dialogue in your mind or on paper with each and every part of you that's not on board the healing train. Help them to see that by "protecting" you, they are actually hurting you and keeping you from getting what you all want—to feel the best you can! Here's a sample inner dialogue:

    > **You:** Does any part of me think that feeling better is a bad idea?

Your resistance: Me! When you are depressed, people empathize with you. Your partner gives you more attention and love when you have depressive episodes. Without this, we might not get the love that we need and crave.

You: Wow, thanks for sharing that with me. I never realized that my depression flared up at just the right moment to get more affection. Knowing this, I can do better to tend to you and love you and give you the warmth and affection we need.

Your resistance: That's all I ever want!

You can repeat this exercise as often as necessary.

CHAPTER 5

MANIFESTING BENEFICIAL RELATIONSHIPS

Life is made up of all kinds of relationships—friendly, romantic, business, and so on. The better your relationships, the better your quality of life. This chapter will help you manifest good relationships with all kinds of great people, depending on your goals. You can call in new friends, clients, a team, a business partner, a therapist—you name it!

As you manifest some new people into your world, remember that...

* They want to connect with you as much as you want to connect with them.
* You add value to people's lives in more ways than one.
* Connection is our number one need as humans.
* Life is made up of relationships.
* Good people are everywhere!

Let's start the exercises. Great people are waiting for you to invite them into your life!

Discover Why You Want New Relationships

Before you call new people into your life, it's important to identify why you need or want this new relationship. Getting clarity on that point will help you make sure you manifest exactly who and what you're looking for. Regardless of the type of relationship you want to experience, there is an underlying need(s) or desire(s) that is waiting to be fulfilled through the relationship. Let's explore what that is with this activity.

1. Ask yourself *why* you want to manifest a new relationship (be it a friend, mentor, business connection, etc.). For example, you might think, *I want to manifest a group of friends in this new city so I can have a sense of community and belonging.*

2. Focus your thoughts, feelings, decisions, actions, and life in a way that helps you to cultivate the feelings you want to experience in this new relationship. To assist you with this, ask yourself these two questions and write down whatever comes to you:
   * What's stopping me from feeling how I want to feel right now?
   * How can I feel more of how I want to feel until the relationship comes?

   For example, you might think, *I only notice how I'm different from others, which makes me feel like I never belong. I could look for ways I am the same as others to feel more like a part of those around me.*

3. Use your discoveries from steps one and two to make empowering adjustments to your daily life so that you can start feeling more of how you want to feel today! Sure, maybe the relationships aren't in place yet, but you can still get creative and feel more of how you want to feel now to make yourself a vibrational match. For example, you could join a volunteer group that shares the same passions as you.

Write Down Your Future Connections

In this exercise, you will be feeling your way into the future and documenting what you notice so as to bring it closer to you than ever before. Grab a pen and your manifesting journal and get ready to write some awesome connections into existence.

Here are a few pointers before you begin your journal entry:

* Write in the *present tense,* as if your dream reality were already a fact.
* Use *specifics* to make it feel more real to you.
* Emphasize how you are *feeling* in this future reality.
* Use a real pen/pencil and paper to write the entry by hand (no typing!).
* Don't limit the Universe by planning exactly *how* and *when* this will all come about.

Suspend all doubt and objection for a few minutes as you write about how you wish your social life to be—but in the present tense, as if you've already got it! Here are some prompts you can use:

* I'm so excited to meet...(e.g., my new business partner)
* I'm thankful to have...(e.g., amazing friends who love and support me)
* I love being able to...(e.g., confidently rely on others in my life)
* I appreciate...(e.g., having a weekly tennis buddy that I can have fun and get a good workout in with)
* I enjoy helping...(e.g., my teammates win)

This exercise can help you feel grateful for the social connections you currently have while also crafting what your ideal social life would look and feel like.

Make Yourself a Match for More Connections via Meditation

As humans, our number one need in life is connection. We are meant to establish bonds, be interdependent, and spend time together to make all of our lives better. This meditation will help you attract more connections. Follow these steps:

1. Sit or lie down comfortably. Close your eyes, lengthen your spine, uncross your limbs, and turn your palms up.
2. Set the intention to connect with people/a person.
3. Imagine you are watching yourself from up above. With each breath, zoom out from the place where you are now. Float your vision to the top of the room, then up above the building. Keep floating up and zooming out to see the neighborhood you're in, then the whole city, then the state/province, the country, the continent, and eventually the whole world! Take a few moments to look at the world from outer space.
4. Take note of all the people on this planet. Now ask for an image of where your people/person are. Imagine that all the people you are meant to connect with start lighting up on the globe.
5. Now connect your energy with theirs by imagining a golden white energy cord extending from where you are to where they are. This energy connects everyone to you. Feel your connection to them. Feel their connection to you.
6. Take several more deep breaths before ending the meditation.

This meditation helps remind you that although for now you may only be energetically connected, soon a physical or virtual connection will follow.

Create a Relationships Vision Board

Healthy relationships add so much value, joy, and support to your life, but sometimes they can be hard to visualize if you haven't experienced or seen examples of what you want from one yet. This exercise will help make those relationship goals more concrete by creating a vision board that focuses on your social connections.

If you're not into paper crafts, don't worry. You can do this online via a *Pinterest* board or digital collage. Also, this is a really fun and powerful activity to do in a group. Have your friends over to create vision boards and then take turns sharing key parts of each one. Here's how to make your relationships vision board:

1. Get a large piece of paper or poster board, glue, scissors, lots of magazines, and any other decorative scrapbooking items.
2. Cut out magazine pictures that represent the types of connections you want to experience. You can also print out your own photos. Use images that make you think, *That's what I want!* They should capture the flavor of connection you are looking for. For example, you might cut out pictures of people who look like they could be your friends, the types of events you might make great connections at, words that define the type of connection you want...anything goes!
3. Place the images and/or words onto your poster board in a fun and creative way that pleases your soul. Rearrange as needed, then glue or tape everything down securely.
4. Finally, hang up your board where you can be inspired by it often. If you don't have anywhere to hang it, tuck it away someplace safe, but take it out periodically to keep your desires in the front of your mind.

This visual reminder of your relationship goals will keep you focused and inspired on your journey to making fulfilling connections.

Write Relationship Affirmations

In this exercise, you'll come up with some mantras and affirmations that you can use to call in new people. No matter how you use them, they will help you manifest those connections!

1. Get out a piece of paper or journal and list some positive, present-tense statements about your future connections. You can start with phrases like:
   * I am...
   * I am open to meeting...
   * I am excited about connecting with...
   * Our relationship is...
   * I feel...

2. Now you can write full affirmations based on these phrases. They can be things that are true now ("I can't wait to make new friends!") or things that will be true when you are experiencing your desired connections ("I love having someone to share my day with"). Here are some affirmations you might write:
   * My social circle is improving.
   * I love my new friends.
   * My friends are super supportive of each other.
   * I am thankful for this helpful relationship.

Once you have your list of affirmations, get creative with how you use them. Meditate on them, affirm them in conversations, repeat them to yourself whenever you feel doubt, or recite them every morning or night as a part of your daily routine. Have fun with it!

Embody Your Inner People Person

Imagine the future version of you who already has all the beneficial relationships you are wanting. What's different about that version of you? What do they do that you don't? What can you do, or stop doing, to activate this future version of yourself today?

In this activity, you'll embody and become this version of you by acting to expand your potential to make connections. Here are some examples of how you can do this, but add as many as you can think of!

* Go to more career networking events/opportunities.
* Find local community and/or service opportunities you're passionate about to meet like-minded people.
* Make it a point to leave your house at least once a day.
* Read books about relating better.
* Keep in touch with important people in your life more often.
* Ask for support when you need it.
* Tell others the types of people you want to connect with.
* Know and own the value that you bring to relationships.

These ideas can help you add action to your energetic work to manifest the relationships you want. Introverts may have a tougher time putting themselves out there, but that's why manifesting is so great—you become the magnet! Just remember that magnets need to be around other magnets in order to come together!

Use Precious Stones to Invite the Right People Into Your Life

No matter what type of relationship you want to create next, there is a stone that can help you do it! In this activity, you'll choose a crystal and activate it to help you call in a special person or people to your life.

1. Pick your "connection crystal." Here are some specific stones that are great for this purpose:
   * Carnelian Stone: a red stone that helps you create whatever you want by increasing your courage and soothing fear and doubt, making it especially great for shy people; also aids in bringing you new resources (a.k.a. new connections).
   * Peridot: great for connecting and celebrating; often called the stone of friendship.
   * Unakite Jasper: helps to promote unity, kindness, and balance.
2. Cleanse your crystal by rinsing it with running water (water straight from nature is best), smudging it (by burning your favorite cleansing plant near it), or burying it in the dirt temporarily. (Some crystals can't get wet, so double-check the best way to cleanse yours ahead of time.)
3. Hold the stone near your heart and mentally or verbally ask it to help you manifest fulfilling relationships. If you're sensitive, you may feel an energetic *yes* response from the stone. You can also meditate with the stone to establish a bond.
4. Charge your crystal by putting it out for a night in the moonlight during the full moon or in full sun during a sunny day.
5. Place your crystal by your front door to amp up the inviting energy or in the relationship corner of your home as shown in feng shui. You could also wear it as jewelry.

Let the amazing powers of crystals help you build strong relationships of all kinds.

Send Friend Requests to the Universe

Just like you would send a friend request on social media, you can send friend requests to the Universe for all your diverse relationship needs! All you need is some paper, a pen, and your relationship-manifesting container. Here's how to do it:

1. Find an envelope to serve as the container for your requests and to represent "sending" those requests out into the world. Keep some sticky notes or small pieces of paper in or near your relationship envelope at all times. Because the feng shui area of the home related to helpful people is in the front, right-hand corner of the home (or any room), it's best to store your envelope somewhere there. Keep in mind, even if you want to hide the envelope for privacy, the feng shui placement will still be helpful.

2. Every time a new relationship desire enters your mind, write it down on one of your small pieces of paper, fold it up, and place it in your envelope. As you do this, set the intention to "set it and forget it." Trust that the Universe is well acquainted with the requests in this envelope, and as soon as you place something in it, the Universe gets to work on it.

3. After some time of collecting your connection wishes—you can wait weeks, months, or years, whatever feels right to you—revisit your envelope and read what you once wanted. Take some time to notice and appreciate how many of your desires for connection came to pass, because they will!

Writing down what you want and keeping those wishes in a dedicated space gives those intentions extra emphasis and energy.

Encourage Connection via Sound Therapy

Everything on earth vibrates with energy. You can tune in to the frequencies of connection and support via sound waves and tap in to the energy present there. Plus, making a playlist of songs will help set your focus on making connections.

Supportive Frequencies

Get in a comfortable position, sitting or lying down, and use headphones to listen to your favorite healing frequencies, specifically ones that will attune you to connection or support. Some of the best frequencies for calling in new people are 639Hz (for harmonious interpersonal relationships) and 432Hz (for heart chakra activation). You can find many free ways to listen to these by searching online. Spend at least ten to twenty minutes breathing deeply as you let the harmonies alter your frequency.

Songs

Make a playlist of at least eight songs specifically designed to help yourself call in the types of people you want in your life. (We'll use eight songs, because the number 8 is sometimes associated with social interactions and general success in life.) Include any and all songs that make you feel how you think you will feel once you have made your connections. Listen to your playlist every day first thing in the morning or the last thing before you go to sleep.

You can repeat these practices daily or as often as you'd like.

Imagine Exciting Relationship Potentials

It's time to exercise one of the most important brain muscles when it comes to manifestation: your imagination! Visualizing what positive relationships look like will help you manifest them in real life. Here's what to do:

1. Take a few moments to breathe and slow down your mind as you set the intention to explore exciting relational potentials for yourself.
2. Close your eyes and imagine that life just handed you the exact type of person or people you've been waiting for. That new best friend, already yours! The investor for your company, arrived! Awesome clients who appreciate working with you, done! How do you feel? What are they like? How is your relationship with them? Why are you thankful for them?
3. Spend some time with these images and feelings in your mind. With a slight smile on your face, imagine all the things you'll do and create together. See and feel how much better your life is with this relationship now in it. How do you work together to make each other's lives better? What do you have to offer each other? How does your connection benefit all parties involved?
4. Keep visualizing this situation in your mind, focusing on the details of how you feel. For as long as you can, go through all the potential positive possibilities, entertaining them one by one for the sake of showing yourself how good things can get. When you do this, you are literally sculpting your future timelines into ones that feel similar to these imaginary moments.

Imagining possibilities in this way not only exercises your imagination—it also readies you to receive what you are asking for. Do this for a few minutes at a time, every day you feel inspired to, and your desired connections will find you fast!

Build Beautiful Relational Boundaries

Not every person will be one of "your people," and that's okay! In this exercise, you'll look to your past to clarify what works for you and what doesn't when it comes to the people in your life. Doing this will help you manifest the best relationship outcomes.

1. Make a quick inventory list of any current relationship complaints. Here are some examples:
   * Not enough friends
   * Flaky people in my life whom I can't count on
   * Lazy coworkers
2. Use your list as a starting point to clarify what you want to create, based on what you already know you don't want anymore. To do that, transform what you wrote into a more positive version. For every item on your list from step one, ask yourself, "What would I rather be experiencing?" Once you've identified what that is (hint: It's usually the opposite of whatever you are currently experiencing), cross off the original problem and replace it with the new desire. For example:
   * "Not enough friends" gets crossed off and becomes "More genuine friends"
   * "Lazy coworkers" becomes "Supportive coworkers/workplace"

What you just clarified are your relational boundaries and preferences. Now you can use this information to your advantage and never settle for less than your new relationship standards. That may mean that some people are no longer a part of your life. That's okay—this will leave space open for new people who are better for you to flow in!

Remind Yourself That It's Safe to Relate

One of the most common blockages people carry when it comes to calling in new people is that they subconsciously feel it's unsafe to depend on others. Somewhere along the line, almost everyone gets hurt in a relationship. Many of us register that memory as a limiting belief that says it's not safe to let others in. Well, today's the day to break free from this or any other forms of false thinking, and open yourself to connection again. This exercise will help you form new beliefs that invite connections instead of block them.

1. Ask yourself: "What limiting or negative beliefs do I have about connecting with others, trusting others, or relating in general?" Remember that you've developed many beliefs from the few times you've been hurt. Write down what comes to mind without judgment. You may think things like:
   * Relationships are too hard.
   * People only care about themselves.
   * Nobody likes me.
   * I don't have anything worthwhile to bring to the table.
   * Friends never stick around.
   * I have to do it all by myself if I want it done right—or at all!
   * Other people just don't get it.
2. Go down your list one by one and question what you've been believing up until this point by asking: Can I know for certain that this is absolutely true/the only truth or possibility (or am I just biased)? Even better, go down your list and argue the opposite perspective, which could be just as true, if not truer! Here's what that might look like:
   * Is it really true that all relationships are too hard? Well, my relationship with my dog is pretty easy; I get along with the neighbors nicely; I've experienced one or two friendships

that were pretty fun. So I guess they aren't all too hard. Maybe they are just too hard when they are with the wrong people and they are actually super easy with the right people.

* Is it 100 percent true that nobody likes me? Technically, no. The door attendant always smiles at me. My spouse loves me. My best friends like me. Wow, there's already a whole list here of people who like me! I'll keep my eyes peeled for more names to add to the list from now on.

* Can I know for certain that people never stick around? Well, so far in my experience this has been mostly true, but that doesn't mean it will always be this way. I see other relationships around me that last. So if it's possible for them, it must be possible for me too.

Doing this exercise on a regular basis will help you dismantle any outdated beliefs that are no longer serving you and replace them with a mindset where you are open to things turning out better this time. Just that slight openness is all it takes to manifest a new outcome!

Get Real with Yourself

If manifesting new people into your life doesn't seem to be happening, it's likely not because there aren't enough good people out there. It's probably because you aren't ready to let them in yet. And that's okay! You can work to be more open, here and now, via some self-reflection in this journaling exercise.

1. Find some quiet alone time and set the intention to get genuinely curious. Take a few moments to release any judgment of yourself and your life. Replace it with a mindset of wanting to understand yourself and your life so as to discover empowering information that will help you better connect with others.

2. Meditate or journal on the following questions:
   * What's been holding me back from experiencing the kind of relationships I want?
   * What can I do differently to improve my connections?
   * What needs am I trying to meet through these desired relationships, and how can I meet them in other ways for now?
   * What am I afraid of when it comes to connecting with others? How can I still grow personal relationships and ensure internal safety at the same time?
   * What am I willing to do, change, or accept in order to feel more connected and supported in general?

Reflecting on these questions can help you recognize patterns and opportunities you might not have seen before. Using this new information, you can make the appropriate changes to your approach. If you are open to trying new things, no matter how challenging they seem at first, you'll reap the rewards!

Upgrade Your Internal Relationships

Because of the Law of Attraction, how healthy and beneficial your relationships with others are will be a direct reflection (to some degree) of the relationships you have with the different parts of yourself. The better you can relate to yourself, the better relationships you'll have in your life. In this exercise, you'll get to know some parts of you and relate to them in a kind and loving way, so as to get all of you on board to manifest new connections.

1. Ask yourself: "Is there any part(s) of me that doesn't want connection/this connection right now or thinks it would somehow be bad for me to get it?"

2. Listen compassionately to any objections or hesitancies that come up. Try to understand how these parts are trying to help you or protect you from *perceived* danger. Keep in mind that it's impossible for you to be against yourself. Whatever comes up is your internal resistance presenting itself to you. Becoming aware of this is so helpful, because now you don't have to stop yourself in unconscious ways and self-sabotaging behavior anymore. Once you know your hesitancies, you can soothe, heal, and overcome them.

3. Open up a dialogue in your mind or on paper with each and every part of you that's not on board with building new relationships. Help them to see that by "protecting" you, they are actually hurting you and keeping you from getting what you all want—this relationship! Here's a sample inner dialogue:

> **You:** Does any part of me think that making new friends is a bad idea?

Your resistance: Me! Remember at your thirteenth birthday how all the kids you thought were your friends didn't even show up because Sally told everyone an untrue rumor about you the day before? Friends are not to be trusted. Why bother? You'll just get hurt again.

You: I hear you. I totally understand how you would think that friends are bad now based on that traumatic experience. I'm sorry that happened to us. Kids can be very mean. But I'm an adult now. And (most) adults are more considerate than that. The chances of something like that happening again are pretty low. So what do you say we at least give some people the opportunity to prove that they can be good friends?

Your resistance: Okay, we'll give some new people a chance, but if they blow it, they are out!

You: Okay, no worries! That's fair.

You can repeat dialogues like this as often as necessary to identify your resistance and try to overcome it.

CHAPTER 6

MANIFESTING HAPPINESS

The pursuit of happiness is a basic human quest. But why chase happiness when you can simply cultivate, encourage, and attract it? The exercises that follow are designed to help you do just that.

As you embark on your happiness-manifesting journey, keep in mind that:

* Everyone deserves to be happy, including you!
* Happiness isn't a destination, but rather an attitude and a lifestyle.
* Happiness is a natural state in the absence of things that block your happiness.
* It's unfair and unrealistic to expect or pressure yourself to feel happy all the time.

* A happy life is made up of many small happy moments.
* Giving yourself permission to be happy is half the battle.

This chapter will help you manifest more happiness, pleasure, enjoyment, fun, and bliss in your life. So let's get started. More happiness awaits!

Add More Happiness and Subtract Unhappiness

At its simplest, manifesting more happiness in your life is a matter of addition and subtraction: Add more thoughts, activities, people, places, and experiences that make you happy and remove as much as you can of what blocks you from feeling happier. In this exercise, you'll apply this equation to your life.

1. Ask yourself: "What are the things that bring me the most joy in life and on a daily basis?" Make a long list and add to it whenever you discover or think of something you enjoy.
   * My cat
   * Long, beautiful drives
   * Spending time with loved ones
   * Creating cool artwork
   * Going to the gym
   * Listening to or making music
   * Reading a good book
   * Relaxing baths
   * Going to the beach
   * A good weekend hike
   * Being good at my job
   * Listening to true-crime podcasts
   * Watching shows that make me laugh
   * A proper date night
   * Helping my kids feel confident
2. Now ask yourself: "What steals and blocks my joy most often?" Make another ongoing list. For example:
   * Worrying about money all the time
   * Not going for what I want
   * My current job
   * Isolating myself

* Not getting enough sleep
* Eating poorly
* Skipping the gym
* Caring too much about what other people think
* Putting extra pressure on myself when I'm already stressed
* Working too many hours a day/week
* Not making time for the things that matter
* Always anticipating the worst

3. Look at both lists and really take in what's working for you and what isn't. How can you focus your thoughts, feelings, decisions, actions, and life in a way that helps you to cultivate more happiness from now on? What are you willing to add and subtract from your life for the sake of your own happiness and fulfillment?

Consider these lists the key to your personal formula for creating a happier life. This may sound too simple to be true, but it's actually quite effective. If you can commit yourself to prioritizing what matters to you and dropping what's no longer serving you, you'll be happier very quickly. Take action on what you have learned and implement changes, big or small, into your life, starting today!

Write Down Your Happiness Specifics

Everyone has a unique version of happiness. Something that might bring you great joy might make someone else miserable, and vice versa. That's why it's important that you bring awareness to the specific things that make you the happiest. In this creative journaling exercise, you'll imagine that if your life were yours to create (which it is!), what exactly would your happiest life look like?

Here are a few pointers before you begin your journal entry:

* Write in the *present tense*, as if your dream reality were already a fact.
* Use *specifics* to make it feel more real to you.
* Emphasize how you are *feeling* in this future reality.
* Use a real pen/pencil and paper to write the entry by hand.
* Don't limit the Universe by planning exactly *how* and *when* this will all come about.

Now imagine your dream life where you are super happy, and write down what it's like as if it were already your reality. How do you spend your time in your most happy life? How do you feel in your most happy life? Here are some phrases you can use to help you:

* My life makes me feel...
* I'm happy that...
* I'm grateful for...
* I light up when I'm...
* My life is full of...

Spend some time describing your happiest life, and soon enough, it will be yours.

Live the Best Day Ever via Meditation

Did you know that your brain can't really tell the difference between reality and your imagination? This is something you can use to your advantage when it comes to manifesting, especially when you want to feel a certain way. Create a happy image in your mind and you'll trick your body into feeling happier. Try it out with this meditation:

1. Sit or lie down comfortably. Close your eyes, lengthen your spine, uncross your limbs, and turn your palms up.
2. Slow down your breath and imagine that you're in your favorite happy place. This could be an imaginary place or a real place. Take in the sights, the sounds, and the smells. Every detail you notice brings joy to your heart.
3. Now imagine that you are here with your favorite person/people in the entire world. Share this happiness with them.
4. As you take in this moment of happiness in your favorite place with your favorite person, imagine that this is only the beginning of the best day of your life. Where do you want to go from here? What will you do on the best day ever? What will you eat on the best day ever? For the next ten to twenty minutes, simply go through the day, step by step, living out the best day ever in your mind. Let your imagination take you for a ride!

Not only will this exercise bring you more enjoyment now, but it will alter your energetic frequency so you can attract more happiness in general later on. Talk about a win-win!

Dream It, Picture It, Live It:
Make a Happiness Vision Board

It's hard not to smile when you see things that make you happy! With this activity, you're going to give yourself a few extra reasons to smile by creating a vision board specifically dedicated to your overall happiness and emotional well-being.

If you're not into paper crafts, don't worry. You can do this online via a *Pinterest* board or digital collage. Also, this is a really fun and powerful activity to do in a group. Have your friends over to create vision boards and then take turns sharing key parts of each one. Here's how to make your happiness vision board:

1. Get a large piece of paper or poster board, glue, scissors, lots of magazines, and any other decorative scrapbooking items.
2. Cut out magazine pictures that represent happiness to you. You can also print out your own photos. Use images that make you think, *That's how I want to feel!* For example, you might cut out pictures of happy people (including yourself!), images of cute baby animals, words and phrases that bring you joy, your favorite food, your favorite places—anything that represents happiness to you.
3. Place the images and/or words onto your poster board in a fun and creative way that pleases your soul. Rearrange as needed, then glue or tape everything down securely.
4. Finally, hang up your board where you can be inspired by it often. If you don't have anywhere to hang it, tuck it away someplace safe, but take it out periodically to keep your desires in the front of your mind.

This visual reminder of your happiness goals will help keep you grateful for the happiness you do have so you can attract more of it!

Write Affirmations to Manifest Happiness

Writing empowering and authentic affirmations will help you activate your joy every time you think, speak, or write them.

1. Get out a piece of paper or journal and list some positive statements that make you happy. You can start with phrases like:
   * I am...
   * I am open to...
   * I am excited about...
   * My life is...
   * I feel...
2. Now you can write full affirmations based on these phrases. They can be things that are true now ("I'm excited to enjoy my life more!") or things that will be true later ("Every day brings me more joy"). Here are some affirmations you might write:
   * I am learning how to be happier every day.
   * I love my support system.
   * I'm excited about all the blessings that I don't even know about yet!
   * I am open to incorporating more joy into every day by scheduling it.
   * I feel fulfilled in life.
   * I can't wait to see how much happiness I can hold in my body without exploding!
   * I am prioritizing my well-being above all else.
   * My feelings matter to me.

Once you have your list of affirmations, get creative with how you use them. Meditate on them, affirm them in conversations, repeat them to yourself whenever you feel doubt, or recite them every morning or night as a part of your daily routine. No matter how you use them, they will support you in becoming a vibrational match to more happiness!

Do a Happiness Inventory

This exercise will take inventory of every single thing in your life that brings a smile to your face. Focusing on what already brings you joy is a great way to invite even more happiness into your life.

For this activity, make a list of all the things that make you happy. Nothing is too big or too small to add to the list. Here are a few examples to get you started:

* I'm thankful for my puppy!
* I love my line of work.
* I'm glad I get to help people.
* Thank you for coffee!
* I love the supportive people in my life.
* I'm excited about my new favorite pair of shoes.
* I enjoy growing my own veggies.

May this list fill your heart as you realize there are so many things to be happy about when you take the time to look for them. After you write everything down, you can thank the Universe for all your current blessings by saying, "Thank you, life, for all these things that bring me joy and happiness!"

Drink Up Some Joy

Everything in the Universe is made up of energy that you can affect. That's what you'll do here—program your drink in order to attune yourself to the energetic frequency of happiness.

1. Choose your drink and pour it into your favorite glass. The more water it contains, the better. (It's best to avoid dehydrators like caffeine and alcohol.) For happiness, it's even more effective if the drink contains some kind of fruit or vegetable that grew in the sun so that it is already charged with lots of bright sunlight energy.

2. With a slight smile on your face, hold the glass in both hands and think of something or someone that makes you incredibly happy or represents happiness to you. As you see it in your mind's eye, project this happy energy into your drink to infuse it with good vibes for at least sixty seconds.

3. Drink up! As you hydrate, you are inviting brightness and joy into your body and mind.

You're now better hydrated and more of a match for happiness and joy than you were a few minutes ago!

Ask Yourself This One Question

A state of happiness is much more attainable when you cultivate it moment by moment, day by day. A person with a happy life isn't happy all the time, but they are generally happy more than they are unhappy. Being happy all the time isn't even possible, but being happy the majority of your life can be a pretty fun goal!

In this exercise, you will ask yourself one question, again and again, for an entire day. And if you like it, keep asking it for the rest of your life!

Sound boring? It's not, because it helps you live your happiest life one decision at a time. Whenever you go to make a decision, no matter how big or small, ask yourself:

"What would bring me the most joy right now or in the long term?"

* When you're deciding what snack to eat, ask yourself, "What snack would bring me the most joy right now?"
* When deciding to go for a walk or go to the gym, ask yourself, "Which activity would bring me the most joy today?"
* When you're thinking about whether you should change your job or not, ask yourself, "What would bring me the most joy in the long term?"

Notice that the question is not, "What would bring my parents the most joy?" "What would bring me the most money?" "What would be the easiest thing to do?" Happiness is not found in these approaches. It is found by doing what's most in alignment for *you* in any given moment. So ask yourself what that is and go with your first instinct.

If you use this question as your new North Star, you'll always come back to more joy—your joy! Eventually, all these moments of going toward your joy will add up to a lifetime of happiness.

Use Crystals to Promote Happiness

Crystals and gemstones hold energy, just like everything else in the Universe. Certain stones are known for properties that can help you manifest happiness. In this exercise, you'll pick a few small happiness stones to keep with you everywhere you go.

1. Pick your "happiness crystal." Anything brightly colored will work. Here are some specific stones that are great for manifesting happiness:
   * Yellow Jasper: a sunny stone that helps encourage optimism and transmute negativity into positivity.
   * Carnelian: helps remove blockages to make room for more confidence, motivation, and joy.
   * Black Tourmaline: the ultimate energy guard that helps protect you from negative energy to maintain your natural light and positive mood.
2. Cleanse your crystal by rinsing it with running water (water straight from nature is best), smudging it (by burning your favorite cleansing plant near it), or burying it in the dirt temporarily. (Some crystals can't get wet, so double-check the best way to cleanse yours ahead of time.)
3. Hold the stone close to your heart and mentally or verbally ask it to help you manifest more happiness. If you're sensitive, you may feel an energetic yes response from the stone. You can also meditate with the stone to establish a bond.
4. Charge your crystal by putting it out for a night in the moonlight during the full moon or in full sun during a sunny day.
5. Keep your stone in your pocket or purse, or wear it on some jewelry to boost your happiness.

Happiness is all around you. Let the natural power of crystals help you connect with it more often.

Tune In to Happiness via Sights and Sound

Like all moods and emotions, happiness is a frequency at its most basic. By connecting with and enjoying frequencies that are happy by nature, you will promote your own happiness to match them.

Sight

Find an image, video, symbol, or sigil that represents happiness, joy, fun, or any similar feeling to you. Maybe it's an image of a smiling baby, the green view from your mountain cabin, or an energy grid that represents the rays of the sun. Pick whatever you like!

For at least eleven minutes, gently gaze at this image in a relaxed and meditative way. As you focus, imagine becoming one with the image. Let it into your psyche so you can really feel the happiness it brings you.

Happy Frequencies

Get in a comfortable position, sitting or lying down, and use headphones to listen to your favorite healing frequencies, specifically ones that will attune you to happiness. One of the best frequencies for happiness specifically is 432Hz. (Many pop songs use this frequency!) You can find many free ways to listen to these by searching online. Spend at least ten to twenty minutes breathing deeply as you let the harmonies alter your frequency.

A Joyful Playlist

Make a playlist of at least eleven songs designed to help yourself feel happy. (We'll use eleven songs because the number 11 has a powerful connection to manifestation.) Include any and all songs that make you feel like you're really enjoying the moment. Listen to your playlist every day first thing in the morning or the last thing before you go to sleep.

You can repeat any of these practices daily or as often as you'd like.

Find Clarity in the Contrast

Sometimes it's the not-so-happy moments that actually inspire you to create stronger happiness down the road. Every time you feel bad, you (consciously or subconsciously) ask for happiness in a more powerful way than ever before. In this exercise, you'll use the power of contrasting experiences to consciously create the happiness you desire.

1. Make a quick list of any areas of your life that are bringing you down and causing unhappiness. These could include a relationship that's expired, a job you no longer want, or any type of stressor in your life right now. For example, you might pinpoint:
   * My toxic relationship
   * This boring job
2. Use your list as a starting to point to clarify what you want to replace it with. For every item on your list, ask yourself, What would I rather be experiencing? Once you've identified what that is (hint: It's usually the opposite of whatever you are currently experiencing), cross off the original problem and replace it with the new desire. For example:
   * "My toxic relationship" gets crossed off and becomes "A healthy and happy relationship"
   * "This boring job" becomes "Work that excites and delights me"

By making and rephrasing this list, you have declared to the Universe what you no longer want to participate in and redefined exactly what you'd like to replace it with. Use this new information to move toward what you want. This process might involve some changing and therefore require some courage, but you can do it!

Question Your Perceived Reality

Your life experience is primarily filtered through your lens of belief. This means that a lot of your suffering doesn't come directly from life circumstances themselves, but rather the painful meanings you assign to them. In this exercise, you'll realize what meanings you have assigned to experiences, and you'll see how those meanings affect your emotions. The happiest people know how to do this, and they do it often so as to choose empowering and beneficial meanings over disempowering ones. Follow these steps:

1. Ask yourself: "What thoughts, stories, or beliefs cause me the most pain right now? What do I make it mean when something bad happens to me?" Take some time to write down whatever comes to you (no matter how ridiculous it looks on paper). Here are some examples of how this might look:
   * Love hasn't worked out for me yet, so that means I'll never be in a loving relationship.
   * I got fired, which means that I suck.
   * My parents put me up for adoption, which means I'm unlovable.
   * I never finished that project, which means that I'm a failure with no follow-through.

   You'll probably notice many of your statements include the word *never* or *always*. This is a good way to spot a powerful assigned meaning!

2. Go down your list one by one, and look at the meanings you've assigned to your hardships. Realize that these meanings are not the absolute truth; they are stories you made up along the way to try and make sense of what went wrong. If these stories cause you disempowerment, it might be time to replace them with a more objective, empowering truth. And that truth

is that something unfortunate happened, but it doesn't have to mean anything bad about you or your life as a whole.

3. Now it's time to assign meanings to these events that help you feel better, not worse. Here are some examples:

   * Love hasn't worked out for me yet, so that means my person is probably still out there!
   * I got fired, which means that wasn't the job for me.
   * My parents put me up for adoption, which could mean many different things about them and what their lives were like at the time.
   * I never finished that project, which means I wasn't really excited about it, so I'll move on to something else.

Notice how the circumstances of the events didn't change, but looking at them through a different lens leaves your mind open to other interpretations of the events. Now you can feel better about what happened and move on to more joyful experiences ahead.

Deal with Sneaky Self-Sabotage

When it comes to manifesting happiness, unintentional self-sabotage can often get in the way. In this exercise, you'll uncover if you have any and then decide what empowering step you can take to not let it hold you back anymore! Now is the time to free your most happy self.

1. Find some quiet time to yourself and set the intention to get genuinely curious. Take a few moments to release any judgment of yourself or your life and replace it with wanting to understand yourself and your life in order to discover empowering information that will help your overall happiness.
2. Meditate or journal on the following questions:
    *   What's been holding me back from experiencing the kind of happiness I want?
    *   What can I do differently to improve my general mood and outlook on life?
    *   What needs must be fulfilled in order for me to be happy?
    *   What am I afraid of when it comes to embracing happiness? How can I still go toward joy and create internal safety at the same time?
    *   What am I willing to do, change, or accept in order to feel more happy and joyous in general?

Feel free to revisit this exercise from time to time to refresh the process and clear any new sabotage that has arisen.

Overcome Internal Resistance to Happiness

Everyone knows the feeling of wanting something while feeling a small part of you that pulls you in another direction. That small part represents the resistance we talked about in Chapter 1. In this exercise, you'll discover if any parts of you think that happiness is potentially threatening, and then deal with this resistance directly in order to create inner resolve and move forward toward your happiest life.

1. Ask yourself: "Is there any part(s) of me that doesn't want to feel happier right now or thinks it would somehow be bad for me to embrace happiness?" (Be honest.)

2. Listen compassionately to any objections or hesitancies that come up. Try to understand how these parts are trying to help you or protect you from *perceived* danger. Keep in mind that it's impossible for you to be against yourself. Whatever comes up is your internal resistance presenting itself to you. Becoming aware of this is so helpful, because now you don't have to sabotage yourself anymore. Once you know your hesitancies, you can soothe, heal, and overcome them.

3. Open up a dialogue in your mind or on paper with each and every part of you that's not truly looking for happiness. Help them to see that by "protecting" you, they are actually hurting you and keeping you from getting what you all want—a happier life! Here's how that dialogue might sound:

> **You:** Does any part of me think that happiness is a bad idea?

> **Your resistance:** Me! The happier you are, the more your friends and family will be jealous of you and not connect with you anymore. Since they are all unhappy, the only way

you can connect with them is in their misery. Lose your misery and you lose your connections.

You: Wow, I never thought about that before. I totally understand this logic. We don't want to lose connection! But maybe there are other happy people out there that we can connect with in our joy and happiness. I would rather connect more with those people anyway!

Your resistance: It's possible. Now that you say that, I'm open to it. I just want connection for us!

Repeat this exercise as often as necessary to keep yourself aware of any internal resistance that could be holding you back.

CHAPTER 7

MANIFESTING PEACE

Locating your inner peace can feel nearly impossible during these fast-moving times! But the good news is that it has always been—and will always be—inside of you, no matter how crazy the circumstances around you are. On the deepest level, there is a rock-solid part of you that's *always* at peace, unwavering in its stillness. The more you can connect with this part of yourself, the more time you can spend in a relaxed state.

As you manifest more peace for your life experience, it's helpful to:

* Stop making "perfect life circumstances" the condition that needs to be met before you give yourself permission to feel peace.
* Embrace peace as an ongoing, ever-evolving practice, and not a finite destination.
* Redesign your life in a way so that you can eliminate as much unnecessary stress as possible. Peace comes easily in the absence of stress.
* Make peace a priority, and you'll naturally make the necessary adjustments required for you to experience more of it.

This chapter has plenty of exercises to get you started on a journey to a more peaceful existence. Enjoy!

Get Specific about What Brings You Peace

It's nice to know that you want more peace (who doesn't?)—but it's even nicer to fully understand *why* you want it and what specifically would help you have more of it. Becoming aware of these personal details is the fastest way to cultivate more peace and calm.

1. Ask yourself *why* you want to manifest more peace. If necessary, keep asking yourself *why* over and over until you narrow it down to a few core feelings and true motivations, then write them down. Here are some possible answers:
   * I want to manifest inner peace so I can feel calm, relaxed, without anxiety, and stress-free.
   * I want to feel calm and relaxed so I can enjoy my days more, focus on what really matters, and be present with my family.
2. Now focus your thoughts, feelings, decisions, actions, and life in a way that helps you to cultivate the feelings you want to experience in your life!

   To assist with this, ask yourself these two questions and write down whatever comes to you:

   * What's stopping me from feeling more peaceful, relaxed, and easy right now?
   * How can I feel more of how I want to feel until I'm generally more relaxed?

   Here are some ways to respond to those questions:

   * Worrying about things I have no control over is preventing my peace.
   * I could feel more peaceful now if I delegated some tasks to others who can help.

* Spending too much time checking emails is really stressing me out and preventing me from being present.
* I think I would feel more relaxed if I spent less time in front of a screen and more time outside getting fresh air!
3. Use your discoveries from steps one and two to make empowering adjustments to your daily life so that you can feel more of how you want to feel today! For example, maybe you could reach out to a coworker and ask if they can help with the email load or turn your phone off in the morning and nighttime as a new personal boundary.

This activity helps you lay out some action steps, but those won't help you much if you don't follow through on them. So begin with these baby steps, and eventually, more and more peace will be yours.

Design Your Peace in Detail in a Journal

When you're finally your most relaxed self with your most peaceful life, it will look and feel certain ways. In this exercise, you'll familiarize yourself with those sensations by daydreaming (in writing) about what your calm future can be.

Here are a few pointers before you begin your journal entry:

* Write in the *present tense,* as if your dream reality were already a fact.
* Use *specifics* to make it feel more real to you.
* Emphasize how you are *feeling* in this future reality.
* Use a real pen/pencil and paper to write the entry by hand (no typing!).
* Don't limit the Universe by planning exactly *how* and *when* this will all come about.

Imagine you are your most peaceful self with your most relaxing life and write down what it will *be* and *feel* like as if it were already your reality. Here are some phrases you can use to help you:

* My days feel easy because...
* I love feeling so...
* It's easy to...
* I'm so glad I don't _____ anymore.
* It's nice to...
* I'm grateful for...
* I'm relaxed knowing that...
* I feel...
* I know that...

With this journal entry, not only are you giving the Universe some specific intel to work with, but you are also spending time focusing on your desire in a positive, nonattached way, which will lead you to create more supportive energy around it! This is one of the most powerful manifestation exercises you can do.

Take Yourself There with Meditation

Peace is our natural state of being in the absence of stress. In this meditation, you'll release some stressors so you can come back to this lighter, calmer state and allow yourself to just "be."

1. Sit or lie down comfortably. Close your eyes, lengthen your spine, uncross your limbs, and turn your palms up. Feel free to use pillows and blankets to help feel comfy, safe, and relaxed. It can also be helpful to lay your arms above your head ("cactus arms" in yoga), a position of surrender. This pose sends signals to the brain that it's okay to relax.

2. Breathe slowly and deeply for a few minutes. With every round of breath, try to breathe more slowly and more deeply, slowing down your heart rate and your thoughts.

3. Imagine that you are in a peaceful natural environment with a slow-flowing river beside you. See how beautiful it is here. Hear the peaceful sounds. Smell the relaxing scents. Feel the relaxing vibes of this place already rubbing off on you. Look around the grounds and take it all in through your senses.

4. As you sit next to this sparkling river, ask it to help take away your problems and stressors. This is a magical healing river, so it will gladly help you out. Then, imagine that every stressor in your life is a small object. Gently place each one on a leaf in the water, and watch it slowly float farther and farther away from you until it disappears downstream. Do this for everything in your life that's stressing you out. Let the river handle these things for you as you watch them drift off and disappear. Repeat this process until you are left without any worries and you've let them all float away.

5. With all your worries now taken care of by the river, just relax here, noticing how it feels to be light and relieved. Notice how

it feels in your body to have given up all your worries. Give yourself permission to just be, enjoy, and replenish. Stay here for as long as you can to expand your tolerance for peace.

Revisit this meditation whenever you're feeling stressed out and need to release some weight from your shoulders. Each time you repeat the meditation, try to spend even more time at the end taking in your peace in the absence of stress. The longer you can go without falling asleep, the better!

Create a Peace Vision Board

Putting the visions of a peaceful life that are currently in your head down on paper will help you focus your energy on making them a reality. In this exercise, you'll make a unique vision board of activities, words, and symbols that feel peaceful to you. Even the process of creating the board can be a peaceful interactive meditation.

If you're not into paper crafts, don't worry. You can do this online via a *Pinterest* board or digital collage. Also, this is a really fun and powerful activity to do in a group. Have your friends over to create vision boards and then take turns sharing key parts of each one. Here's how to make your own peace vision board:

1. Get a large piece of paper or poster board, glue, scissors, lots of magazines, and any other decorative scrapbooking items.
2. Cut out magazine pictures that represent the type of peace you want to experience. You can also print out your own photos. Use images that make you think, *That's the vibe I'm going for!* They should capture the flavor of the calm you want to experience. For example, you might cut out a picture of someone enjoying a beach sunset, a relaxing reading nook, a mug of tea, a sloth that represents moving slowly, someone getting a massage or facial, and so on.
3. Place the images and/or words onto your poster board in a fun and creative way that pleases your soul. Rearrange as needed, then glue or tape everything down securely.
4. Finally, hang up your board where you can be inspired by it often. If you don't have anywhere to hang it, tuck it away someplace safe, but take it out periodically to keep your desires in the front of your mind.

This visual reminder of what peace looks like to you will foster more calming energy around and within you.

Give Yourself Permission to Feel Peaceful

So often we can't relax because we don't give ourselves *permission* to. We use being in a constant state of stress as an attempt to motivate ourselves to get things done. But as Chinese philosopher Lao Tzu once said, "Nature does not hurry, yet everything is accomplished." Time to take a hint from nature and switch up your approach!

1. Get out a piece of paper or journal and list some positive, present-tense statements about embracing your peace. You can start with phrases like:
   * I am...
   * I am open to...
   * It is soothing to know that...
   * My life is...
   * I feel...
   * I give myself permission to...
   * It is safe to...

2. Now you can write full affirmations based on these phrases. They can be things that are true now ("I intend to create a more peaceful life") or things that will be true later ("My life is more peaceful than ever before"). Here are some affirmations you might write:
   * I am learning how to be calmer every day.
   * I am eliminating unnecessary stress from my life.
   * I am open to feeling more relaxed than I have before.
   * It is soothing to know that I don't have to rush my life.
   * I feel relaxed.
   * All I have is time.
   * I'm letting go of the pressures I place on myself.
   * I love this feeling of ease and grace.
   * I give myself permission to rest.

* It's okay to relax.
* It is safe to take a break.
* Calm is my natural state of being.

You can use these calming statements often to help fortify your peace as you journey inward to find it. Recite them every morning in the mirror to start your day off on a peaceful note, or meditate on them before bedtime to transition into a calm bedtime state.

Add Peaceful Moments to Your Day

In order to manifest more peace, you can begin by embodying peace little by little in your daily life. This can be easier said than done, but if you break it down into bite-sized pieces, you can do it! In this exercise, create a road map for how to become your own version of the peaceful Buddha.

1. Imagine that you've been granted the wish of peace and now you're a super peaceful person. Think about how this version of yourself is different from you now. Start by asking yourself the question: If I were already my most peaceful self, how would I think, talk, and act?

2. Next, write down what comes up for you. For example, you might think, *If I were already my most peaceful self, I would...*
   * Trust my future more.
   * Be great at meditation.
   * Walk around with a lighter step.
   * Take my time going through my day instead of rushing everywhere.
   * Speak more slowly and clearly.
   * Count my blessings instead of my stressors before bed.
   * Support my body with herbs that promote relaxation.

3. Now, try to implement the ideas that feel most accessible from your list. Even though you might not actually be a super peaceful person *yet*, you can embrace more peace in more moments by channeling the most peaceful version of you.

Practice makes perfect, and this activity helps you identify small ways that you can practice being peaceful until it becomes second nature to you.

Infuse Your Drinking Water with Peace

All matter holds energy, and water is no different. In this exercise, you'll program a drink to contain peaceful intentions to promote the calm you seek.

1. Choose your drink and pour it into your favorite glass. The more water it contains, the better. (It's best to avoid dehydrators like caffeine and alcohol.) For peace, something calming is best (like an herbal tea).
2. Relax your body, face, and breath as you hold the glass in both hands and think of something that brings you calm. This could be a soothing mantra you've recently created, a special relaxing place, someone who makes you feel safe, or anything that represents peace to you. As you see it in your mind's eye, project this peaceful energy into your drink to infuse it with these good vibes for at least sixty seconds.
3. Slowly but deliberately sip away! As you hydrate, you are making yourself an energetic match to the frequencies of peace and harmony.

Drinking this programmed water will help your body prepare to receive the peace the Universe will no doubt send you.

Use Crystals to Support Your Inner Peace

Perhaps one of the most famous benefits of healing crystals is that they can be used to help encourage more inner peace and calm. In this exercise, you'll use whatever peaceful stones you feel a personal connection to and ask them to help you out with this goal.

1. Pick your "zen stone." Anything that looks or feel soothing to you is best, but here are some ideas:
   * Blue Lace Agate: a visually soothing stone that helps calm the mind.
   * Black Tourmaline: helps remove tension, stress, and bad vibes so you can come back to peace.
   * Sodalite: often called the stone of peace, it can even help to soothe during panic attacks because it is so relaxing.
2. Cleanse your crystal by rinsing it with running water (water straight from nature is best), smudging it (by burning your favorite cleansing plant near it), or burying it in the dirt temporarily. (Some crystals can't get wet, so double-check the best way to cleanse yours ahead of time.)
3. Hold the stone near your heart and mentally or verbally ask it to help you connect to your inner peace. If you're sensitive, you may even feel an energetic *yes* response from the stone. You can also meditate with the stone to establish a bond.
4. Charge your crystal by putting it out for a night in the moonlight during the full moon or in full sun during a sunny day.
5. Wear your crystal on your body to help keep the calm vibes coming all day, meditate with it, or sleep with it under your pillow to promote peace.

Crystals can help with many spiritual quests, but they are especially effective at promoting peace. Connect with one today to help bring you back to your calm.

Find Peace Through Safety

If you *always* base your peace on outer circumstances, it's going to be hard to find it, let alone keep it. But in some instances, it is actually helpful to notice the things around you that *do* bring you peace, and these are usually associated with personal safety. In this exercise, you'll take inventory of what makes you feel safe so you can bring yourself into a state of calm.

1. Grab a pen/pencil and your journal. Title your journal entry something like "Things That Bring Me Peace."
2. Spend some time listing all the things, people, and places in your life that bring you peace. Here are some examples:
   * The shining sun
   * My morning chamomile tea
   * Good people in the world
3. Add another section to this journal entry for a new list called "Reasons Why I'm Safe."
4. List all the reason why you are safe right here, right now. To do this, finish the sentence "I am safe because _____." Notice how you feel when you realize how safe you are. Here are some sample answers:
   * My fridge is full of food.
   * My bills have already been paid this month.
   * I have people in my life who love me and support me.
5. Review your lists and breathe in and out, focusing on these things that are supporting your peace.

These lists can bring you a moment of gratitude and appreciation for what is helping you in this life. Acknowledging the peace and calm you do have will help you manifest more of it.

Activate Peace via Sound Therapy

You can easily cultivate more peace when you allow your senses to get involved! A relaxing candle or calming image can be helpful to engage your sense of sight or smell, but in this exercise, you'll use your ears to listen to peaceful frequencies in order to attune yourself to more inner peace whenever and wherever you want.

Calm Frequencies

Get in a comfortable position, sitting or lying down, and use headphones to listen to your favorite healing frequencies, specifically ones that will attune you to peace and calmness. Some of the best frequencies for promoting peace and harmony are 432Hz and 528Hz. You can find many free ways to listen to these by searching online. Spend at least ten to twenty minutes breathing deeply as you let the harmonies alter your frequency.

Songs

Make a playlist of at least twenty-two songs specifically designed to help calm yourself. (We'll use twenty-two songs because the number 2 represents balance and harmony, and double twos is double the balance!) Include any and all songs that make you feel relaxed, calm, soothed, or peaceful. Listen to your playlist every day first thing in the morning or the last thing before you go to sleep.

You can practice these exercises daily or as often as you like.

Engage in Peaceful Breathing

How you breathe is a direct reflection of how calm and regulated your body is at any given moment. It also works the other way around: You can use your breath as a tool to intentionally cultivate more calm and nervous system regulation. Try this breathing exercise as a part of your daily routine and see how it positively affects your nervous system.

1. Sit in a comfortable seat, close your eyes, and place your full attention on your breath. Notice if it is shallow or deep, fast or slow. Take inventory of your relaxation or stress level in this moment so you can see how/if it has changed or improved later.

2. As you take a nice long, slow breath in, spell out the letters *p-e-a-c-e* in your mind. Hold your breath for one moment. Then, as you exhale a long, slow breath, recite the same letters again in your mind. You will spell *peace* as you breathe in and spell *peace* again as you breathe out. This will help you focus on peace and help you slow down your breathing simultaneously. Repeat this pattern for at least ten rounds of breath. With each round of breath, slow down how quickly you spell out the letters, making each round deeper and longer.

Check back in with your nervous system and notice if you feel more calm, open, or relaxed afterward. Even if you feel just a little bit better, it's a win! And feel free to keep going for even more effect.

Transform Stress Into Calm

In this exercise, you'll explore how to make your life more peaceful by making it less stressful. After all, as we've explored before, peace is what's left in the absence of stress. Can you rid yourself of *all* stressors? No. But can you minimize stress and get rid of unnecessary stress? Yes! This exercise will help you reduce the number of stressors in your life to do just that.

1. Write down a list of any current stressors in your life. These can be daily things that stress you out or bigger-picture areas of your life that you find generally stressful. Don't spend so much time making your list that you make yourself anxious thinking about all your stressors—spend just enough time to notice what's causing issues for you. Here are some sample answers:

   * Picking up my kids from school while I'm working
   * All the dysfunction in the world
   * Constantly obsessing about my weight

2. Use your list as a starting point for ways that you could make your life more peaceful. For each item on your list, ask yourself, "What would I rather be experiencing?" "Can I eliminate or delegate this thing so it's not as stressful to me?"

3. Once you've identified what you would rather be experiencing and what you could do now or later to alleviate some stress, cross off the original problem and replace it with the new desire and solutions that came up. For example:

   * "Picking up my kids from school while I'm working" gets crossed off and becomes "Ask my partner if they can pick up on Wednesdays."

* "All the dysfunction in the world" becomes "A more peaceful world. I can live my life in peace to contribute to the collective peace."
* "Constantly obsessing about my weight" becomes "Focusing on eating the good foods that I enjoy and limiting my weigh-ins to once a month for health purposes only."

By adjusting these items to be less stressful, you have declared to the Universe what you no longer want to participate in, and you've redefined exactly what you'd like to replace it with. Use this new information to alter your thoughts, habits, decisions, and actions to support yourself in lessening your stress levels and creating more opportunities for peace.

Make Peace with Your Stress

While you can't always change the stressful circumstances of your life, you can change your *perspective* and the *stories* you create about those circumstances. In this exercise, you'll discover what it feels like to make peace with your stress, maybe for the first time ever.

1. Go back to the list of things that are stressing you out from the previous exercise (Transform Stress Into Calm) or create a new one.
2. Identify the items on your list that you can't really change.
3. For each one of these unchangeable stressors, tell yourself that it is *okay* that things are how they are right now. Cultivate acceptance of your current reality so as to release resistance to it. Make it acceptable that life is stressful sometimes. For example, you could say to yourself:
   * My bills are stressing me out right now...and that's okay.
   * My family is stressing me out right now...and that's okay.
   * Work is stressing me out right now...and that's okay.
   * It's okay to be stressed! It's a natural part of life sometimes.
4. Take several deep breaths as you work to accept your current situation. Feeling that it's wrong to be stressed can make the problem worse! Let go of that resistance, and you'll find more peace enter your life, even if those difficult circumstances haven't changed yet.

The important thing to remember is that stress and stressors, like all things in life, are temporary, and that it's okay to get stressed out because that means you're a human and that you *care*! What if instead of making yourself feel wrong or bad for worrying, you made yourself feel right and beautiful for caring in the first place?

Align Your Energy to Promote Peace

Sometimes there are parts within you that feel that being without peace is somehow serving you or meeting a need. When this happens, it's harder to manifest peace, because parts of you are working against this goal behind the scenes. In this exercise, you'll see if this is happening to you and create some internal resolve in order to get all (instead of just some) your parts working toward peace. Here's how:

1. Ask yourself: "Is there any part(s) of me that doesn't want peace right now or thinks it would somehow be bad for me to get it?"

2. Listen compassionately to any peace objections or hesitancies that come up. Try to understand how these parts are trying to help you or protect you from *perceived* danger. Keep in mind that it's impossible for you to be against yourself. Whatever comes up is your internal resistance presenting itself to you. Becoming aware of this is so helpful, because now you don't have to sabotage yourself anymore. Once you know your hesitancies, you can soothe, heal, and overcome them.

3. Open up a dialogue in your mind or on paper with each and every part of you that's wary of peace for some reason. Help them to see that by "protecting" you, they are actually hurting you and keeping you from getting what you all want—peace! Here's how that dialogue might look:

> **You:** Does any part of me think that inner peace is a bad idea?

> **Your resistance:** Me! When you are relaxed, you don't seem motivated to get anything done. I think it's best for you to stay stressed so you stay motivated.

You: Interesting. Thanks for sharing. I understand how you would think that my feeling more peaceful could lead to less "doing." But the truth is, if I'm more peaceful I'll actually be able to better focus on doing the things that are important, and I'll do them in a relaxed and effective way instead of rushing to stay busy for the sake of feeling productive. See the difference?

Your resistance: Yes. We are addicted to *doing*. But maybe relaxing more and then doing from that space could work better and still get things done.

You: Exactly! Glad we are on the same page now.

You can repeat this process as often as necessary to identify and overcome any new resistance that arises.

CHAPTER 8

MANIFESTING PURPOSE

This chapter will help you discover and clarify your purpose. This could refer to your purpose (or purposes) in general, such as a mission statement for your life, or it could be your purpose as it applies to, say, your work or career. Either way, the exercises that follow will help empower you to live more in alignment with your purpose than ever before.

As you embark on living a more purposeful life, it's best to keep in mind that:

* Your purpose gets to be whatever you want it to be!
* You came into this life for many reasons, not just one single purpose.
* Your purpose doesn't always have to be tied to a career, though it often does overlap when living in alignment.
* The quickest way to find your purpose is to follow your joy and be courageous enough to care about how you feel above all else.

"Finding your purpose" doesn't have to be intimidating or overwhelming. Think of it as simply discovering or reconnecting with what you're already passionate about. Let's try these exercises—a more aligned life is calling!

Distinguish What Your Purpose Looks and Feels Like

The great news about your life and your purpose is that you get to *choose* what it is, and you don't have to pick just one! At some level, before you were even born, you chose to come to this earth for *many* different purposes—to discover the world, to live the human experience, to play, to create, to love, to laugh—and on a conscious level, today, you can choose what you want your life to be about. Doing this will help you and the Universe better direct your life in a way that makes you feel lit up and excited to do whatever you decide to do!

1. Instead of waiting for your purpose to "find" you, take a more proactive approach and ask yourself what you *want* your purpose(s) in this life to be. After all, it's your life—you get to do whatever you want to do with it! If you could choose anything (which you can), what would that be? Don't limit yourself to just one. Write down all the purposes that feel good to you. For example:
   * I want my purpose to be helping young women with depression.
   * My purpose is to help the people around me.
   * I'm here to contribute my ideas and unique perspective to the world.
2. Then ask yourself *why* you want that to be your purpose, and narrow it down to a few core feelings.
   * I want to help young women with depression to make the world a happier place. Then I'll feel good knowing that more people are happier because of me.
   * I want to help people around me so I can feel like a valuable and contributing member of my community.

* I want to contribute my ideas and perspectives to the world because I know I have good ones that might interest, entertain, or teach others.

Doing this exercise will help you discover what you want your life to be about and why so that you can understand your intentions for being here. Then you can much more easily live in alignment with them. And the best part? If you pick something that you don't end up loving as much as you thought you would, you can pick again! Who says your life had to have only one purpose forever and ever? Who says you can't evolve and change as you go?

Align with Your Purposeful Future

Imagine you were already living your most aligned, purposeful life. In this exercise, you'll align with your future as it pertains to your purpose by daydreaming about it on paper.

Here are a few pointers before you begin your journal entry:

* Write in the *present tense*, as if your dream reality were already a fact.
* Use *specifics* to make it feel more real to you.
* Emphasize how you are *feeling* in this future reality.
* Use a real pen/pencil and paper to write the entry by hand.
* Don't limit the Universe by planning exactly *how* and *when* this will all come about.

Now imagine your dream life where you are already living out your purpose. Write down what it will be like as if it were already your reality. Here are some phrases you can use to help you:

* My life makes me feel...
* My work matters, and it helps people...
* I love _____ about doing _____.
* I'm happy that I get to contribute in these ways...
* I'm grateful for a life where I get to...
* I'm here to...
* I enjoy...

When you do this, not only are you giving the Universe some specific intel to work with, but you are also spending time focusing on your desire in a positive, nonattached way, which will lead you to create more supportive energy around it. Do this often and you'll be unstoppable.

Ask Your Future Self

At times you may feel unclear about your purpose, and that's okay. Luckily there's a part of you that can help with this! That part of you is your future, or higher, self. However you want to label it, it can bring you some clarity. All you have to do is ask!

1. Sit or lie down comfortably. Close your eyes, lengthen your spine, uncross your limbs, and turn your palms up.
2. Breathe slowly and deeply for a few minutes, setting the intention to connect with your higher self or future self, whichever resonates more with you.
3. As you sit and breathe with your eyes closed, see in your mind's eye some fog at a distance in front of you. You notice a figure emerging from this fog and slowly walking toward you. As they come into focus you realize that it's you (your higher self or a future version of you). Let them come close so you can ask them whatever you want to know: "What is my purpose? What's going to light me up the most in this life? What have I come here to do?" Listen to whatever they have to say. Take in your own wisdom and knowledge. Whenever you are done communicating with this part of you, thank them for the guidance and then see yourself merging with them as two bodies melt into one. Know that you have now connected with the part of you that is connected to your purpose, and hence you are more connected to your purpose than before.

See Your Purpose in Pictures

The fastest way to make your purpose fall into your lap is to follow what feels good for you. Your passion and your joy will always lead you right to your purpose, because your purpose will always feel fulfilling and energizing to you. In this activity, you'll create a vision board of images that light you up so as to manifest your purpose through pictures!

If you're not into paper crafts, don't worry. You can do this online via a *Pinterest* board or digital collage. Also, this is a really fun and powerful activity to do in a group. Have your friends over to create vision boards and then take turns sharing key parts of each one. Here's how to make your purpose vision board:

1. Get a large piece of paper or poster board, glue, scissors, lots of magazines, and any other decorative scrapbooking items.
2. Cut out magazine pictures that represent your personal passions and joys. You can also print out your own photos. Use images that make you think, *That's what I want my life to be about!* They should capture the flavor of your ideal life and purpose. For example, you might cut out images of hobbies or activities you enjoy, words that describe the kinds of contributions you like to make, or pictures of you in your element or a flow state.
3. Place the images and/or words onto your poster board in a fun and creative way that pleases your soul. Rearrange as needed, then glue or tape everything down securely.
4. Finally, hang up your board where you can be inspired by it often. If you don't have anywhere to hang it, tuck it away someplace safe, but take it out periodically to keep your desires in the front of your mind.

This vision board will help remind you of what types of things represent your most authentic self.

Affirm Your Purpose Through Words

In this exercise, you'll create some encouraging statements that get you pumped about how to spend your time and your life. Words are powerful, and writing statements that support your purpose will help you live it every day.

1. Get out a piece of paper or journal and list some positive, present-tense statements about your life and your purpose. You can start with phrases like:
   * I am...
   * I am open to...
   * I am excited about...
   * My purpose is...
   * I am here to...
   * I feel...
   * I'm passionate about...

2. Now you can write affirmations based on these phrases. They can be things that are true now ("I'm excited to discover what I want to do in this life!") or things that will be true later ("I have clarity in what I offer to myself and the world"). Here are some affirmations you might write:
   * My purpose is to play!
   * I get to do whatever I want to do with my life.
   * I live powerfully in my purpose.
   * My passions guide my life.
   * I am open to being surprised by what my true purpose is.
   * I am willing to try different things until something sticks.
   * I came here for many good reasons.
   * I add value to the world no matter what my purpose is.

Once you have your list of affirmations, get creative with how you use them. Meditate on them, affirm them in conversations, repeat them to yourself whenever you feel doubt, or recite them every morning or night as a part of your daily routine. There are no right or wrong purposes, so write and repeat whatever feels authentic to you.

Share Your Dreams with Helping Hands

Now that you've gained some clarity around what you want your purpose to look and feel like, it's time to share it with a friend! In this exercise, whenever the next organic opportunity arises, you'll share your purpose and your dream with someone who might be able to help! The Universe loves to work through other people to help you get where you want to go. So create that opportunity by vocalizing your dreams to the people around you who will get it!

The next time you find yourself in a conversation with someone who supports you, bring up what you've discovered about your purpose and share any ideas or insights about how you want to spend your life. Share with the intention of being seen, heard, and helped! People who love you will love helping you. Your friend may know someone who can help you better live out your purpose. A family member might know of an opportunity to do what you want to do. They may even have some ideas about where your talents lie and how you could implement them.

The goal is to unapologetically own what you want your purpose to be and put feelers out there for any support from the Universe. Whether or not someone else can help, you will benefit energetically from speaking about what you want to experience. And who knows? Maybe the people around you will be able to support you in some unexpected way. Regardless, speak those dreams into existence!

Become Your Future Self

Earlier you met up with your future/higher self to gain some insight. Now you'll put some of that insight into action and *become* your future self—now, through daily activities that line up with or lead you to your purpose! If you want to manifest your purpose, the fastest way to do it is to follow what feels good to you and let your passion lead the way.

What can you do now to help put yourself into a state of joy or passion, which will ultimately guide you toward your purpose? For this activity, make a list of any and all things that make you feel happy to be alive, and then do at least one of them every day. Here are some examples of how to do this, but get creative in however you want to practice joy and passion:

* Helping my kids get ready for the day
* Making food for my loved ones
* Practicing archery
* Playing the piano
* Going on long runs
* Standing up for what I believe is right
* Volunteering at my church
* Enjoying a great movie on the couch
* Teaching others how to _____

The more passion and joy you exude, the faster your purpose will fall right into your lap and the more you'll be in alignment with your purpose in general.

Infuse Yourself with Intention

Now that you have a good idea of what you have chosen as your purpose during this time or for your life in general, you can program a drink to help you embody it! Intention is everything when it comes to what you put in your body. Infuse your drink with your intentions before you consume it, and they will be that much easier to manifest!

1. Choose your drink and pour it into your favorite glass. The more water it contains, the better. (It's best to avoid dehydrators like caffeine and alcohol.)
2. Hold the glass in both hands and think about your desired purpose. Even if you don't know exactly what you want it to be, you can at least focus on the flavor of what it will be like. For at least sixty seconds, cultivate this feeling of your purpose with pure positive focus, and then imagine yourself infusing your drink with this energy. Picture this energy literally changing and upgrading the composition of your drink. Water is energetically very impressionable, so you may be upgrading its energetic makeup with your thoughts when you do this.
3. Drink up! As you hydrate, you are harmonizing with your purpose and raising the frequency of your body simultaneously.

As you take in this drink charged with intention, your body will have to shift its energy in order to hold the high-frequency liquid. Talk about a vibrational hack!

Identify the Best Crystals for Your Direction

Plenty of stones are ready and waiting to help you cultivate and align with your purpose. This activity will help you choose and activate the best one for you.

1. Pick your "purpose crystal." Here are some specific stones that are great for supporting this goal:
   * Hematite: a root and sacral chakra stone that helps give you the confidence to go for what you want with self-esteem, support, and groundedness.
   * Moonstone: an intuition-enhancing stone that will shine a light on the pathway back to your true self.
   * Tiger's Eye: a powerful manifestation stone that helps you direct your energy in the most rewarding way.
2. Cleanse your crystal by rinsing it with running water (water straight from nature is best), smudging it (by burning your favorite cleansing plant near it), or burying it in the dirt temporarily. (Some crystals can't get wet, so double-check the best way to cleanse yours ahead of time.)
3. Hold the stone near your heart and mentally or verbally ask it to help you more deeply align with your purpose. If you're sensitive, you may even feel an energetic *yes* response from the stone. You can also meditate with the stone to establish a bond.
4. Charge your crystal by putting it out for a night in the moonlight during the full moon or in full sun during a sunny day.
5. Place your crystal next to your vision board, wear it as jewelry, sleep with it by your bed, or meditate with it often.

Let the crystal you choose remind you and inspire you to live your passion every day.

Empower Your Purpose with Sound

Depending on what your specific purpose is, you can enhance the energy of it by listening to empowering and healing frequencies. This is one of the easiest ways to program yourself for success when it comes to living more in alignment with what you came here to do!

Frequencies to Help You Find Your Purpose

Get in a comfortable position, sitting or lying down, and use headphones to listen to your favorite healing frequencies, specifically ones that will attune you to your purpose. Two of the best frequencies for finding your purpose specifically are 396Hz (liberates you from guilt and fear) and 741Hz (aids in creating solutions and amplifying self-expression). You can find many free ways to listen to these by searching online. Spend at least ten to twenty minutes breathing deeply as you let the harmonies alter your frequency.

Songs

Make a playlist of at least twenty songs specifically designed to help yourself manifest or live out your purpose. Include any and all songs that make you feel passionate or joyful about life and what you are doing with yours! Listen to your playlist every day first thing in the morning or the last thing before you go to sleep.

You can repeat either of these exercises daily or as often as you'd like.

Use Your Contrast to Bring Clarity

Ironically, you can usually find out what you came here to experience by looking at the contrast of your life. We cannot know and appreciate what we *do* want without first becoming familiar with what we *don't* want. In this exercise, you'll explore some of your contrast and see if it leads you to a purpose or several purposes that are your unique missions here on earth!

1. On a piece of paper, journal about painful or unwanted patterns that have happened to you in the past or are happening now. This will identify the contrast of your life. For example, maybe you experienced:
   * Significant examples of abandonment from a young age
   * Lots of lack in your life
2. After you've identified some personal themes of yours, take time to think about and write down what the opposite of each would be. What would you rather be experiencing? What experience would help you heal from the past? This is all a part of your purpose/purposes! For example, you might realize:
   * Because you experienced abandonment, your purpose might be to experience connection, acceptance, and relationships that have longevity.
   * Because you experienced lack, your purpose could be to experience abundance in all forms.
3. Take this knowledge into your being and realize that you are meant to experience the opposite of whatever hurt you or upset you. Usually our biggest struggles are our biggest opportunities for mastery! The Universe wants things to come full circle for you. Your purpose is to graduate out of whatever cycles you've been in and experience your desires in full.

Let Go of Old Stories

You may find sneaky limiting beliefs and outdated stories hiding in your psyche that are preventing you from finding your purpose. In this exercise, you'll identify what those are for you and rework them so they no longer hold you back.

1. Ask yourself: "What limiting or negative beliefs do I have about my purpose?" Then take some time to write down whatever comes to you (no matter how ridiculous it looks on paper).
   * I don't have a purpose.
   * I have nothing to contribute to the world.
   * All I want to do is be a good dad.
   * My career doesn't reflect my purpose.
   * I don't want to commit to just one mission, I came here to do it all!
   * I don't know how to execute my purpose.

2. Go down your list one and by one and question what you've been believing up until this point by asking: Can I know *for certain* that this is absolutely true/the only truth or possibility (or am I just biased)? You can also play with this statement: "What if it wasn't wrong that..." Even better, go down your list and argue the opposite perspective, which could be just as true, if not truer! For example:
   * Can I know for certain that I have nothing to contribute to the world? Well, I might not be super talented at any one thing in particular, but I must be here for a reason, otherwise I wouldn't even exist!
   * What if it wasn't wrong that all I want to do is be a good dad? Maybe that is my purpose since that is what I'm the most passionate about. It's beautiful to help raise little humans—that's a worthwhile purpose!

* What if it wasn't wrong that I don't want to tie myself to just one purpose? I'm here to execute many purposes and experience many things!

Time to let go of what's been holding you back up until this point. Reframe how you see yourself and your life!

Reflect On Your Path

Guess what? It's almost impossible for you to be off your path. And if you did somehow manage to do it, your life would keep rerouting you to get you back on track. In this exercise, you'll do some self-inquiry as it pertains to your purpose so you can further release any blockages and fully embrace whatever you came here to do in this life.

1. Find some quiet time to yourself and set the intention to get genuinely curious. Take a few moments to release any judgment of yourself and replace it with wanting to understand yourself and your life so as to discover empowering information that will help you live your purpose.
2. Meditate or journal on the following self-reflective questions:
   * If money were no object, how would I spend the majority of my time?
   * What's been holding me back from following my passions and pursuing what lights me up?
   * What can I do differently in order to follow my joy more?
   * What am I afraid of when it comes to my purpose? How can I still go toward my purpose and create internal safety at the same time?
   * What am I willing to do, change, or accept in order to live more in alignment with what I came here to do?
   * What would I do if I knew I was destined to succeed at it?

Your path may not be a straight line, but that doesn't mean it's not the right path for you. The Universe knows what you need.

Integrate All of You

It's important to get all your internal parts working together to help you best live out your purpose. If any parts of you aren't yet ready for this step, for whatever reason (which you will soon discover), you'll be able to address that here so as to create internal resolve. After this exercise, you'll be able to more fully embrace your purpose.

1. Ask yourself: "Is there any part(s) of me that doesn't want to (insert purpose here) right now or thinks it would somehow be bad for me to pursue/do?"

2. Listen compassionately to any objections or hesitancies that come up. Try to understand how these parts are trying to help you or protect you from *perceived* danger. Keep in mind that it's impossible for you to be against yourself. This is your internal resistance presenting itself to you. Becoming aware of this is so helpful, because now you don't have to sabotage yourself anymore. Once you know your hesitancies, you can soothe, heal, and overcome them.

3. Open up a dialogue in your mind or on paper with each and every part of you that's not on board the purpose train. Help them to see that by "protecting" you, they are actually hurting you and keeping you from getting what you all want—to follow your passions and live out your purpose! Here's a sample inner dialogue:

> **You:** Does any part of me think that traveling the world is a bad idea?
>
> **Your resistance:** Me! The world is a dangerous place with lots of bad people in it. You can't just go everywhere and anywhere—it's not safe!

You: I hear you. I appreciate your concern and understand where you're coming from. I know there is danger and evil out there, but there is also beauty and adventure out there! I will do everything I can to minimize any risks and to plan out the safest trips that I can!

Your resistance: All right, if you can make it as safe as possible, I'll be more okay with it.

Repeat as often as necessary.

INDEX

make TIME FOR you!

PICK UP OR DOWNLOAD YOUR COPIES TODAY!